ELECTRIC SKILLET COOKBOOK
Complete

Big Mouth Watering
Recipes for your
Best Rated BPA Free
Nonstick Energy Saving
Cookware

By: Shannon McMillian

Shannon McMillian

HLR Press
Southern California

LEGAL NOTICE

WANT FREE BOOKS?... ABSOLUTELY!

OUR NEW BOOKS SENT TO YOUR EMAIL MONTHLY

For our current readers...if you like receiving free books to add to your collection, then this is for you! This is for promoting our material to our current members so you can review our new books and give us feedback when we launch new books we are publishing! This helps us determine how we can make our books better for you, our audience! Just go to the url below and leave your name and email. We will send you a complimentary book about once a month.

Get My Free Book

www.HealthyLifestyleRecipes.org/FreeBook2Review

INTRODUCTION

This book will show you why this safe nonstick cookware is the only skillet you should have in your kitchen to cook with! If you've recently purchased a non-stick titanium skillet or frying pan, then this book can quickly give you the expertise you need to fully enjoy the benefits of nonstick cuisine. This book was written for today's reader with quick, short paragraphs. There are also plenty of illustrations and easy-to-understand instructions. And, with 99 delicious and popular recipes at your fingertips, you'll always have a healthy meal ready for guests and family. In this book, you will also learn: How to choose the best nonstick skillet. How to clean your nonstick cookware and take care of it, A history of non-stick pan cookware, Pro-tips to help you excel in the kitchen and over 99 popular and deliciously healthy recipes to choose from!

We've also included *(just for you)* in this book a new "Bonus Section" for mouthwatering Marinades! So, if you want your meat to be this amazingly "High Flavored, Smack in the Mouth" taste that you've never experienced before...then we have "this bonus section" for you to enjoy! These are our 10 favorite marinades that we pulled out of "Our Play Book" just for you! Every pulsating taste of bliss that you'll ever want on your meats is right here at your fingertips!

"Now it's time to impress, not only your peers, but yourself with these delicious, unique recipes and meat soaking, mouthwatering marinades!" Enjoy! ~ Shannon McMillian :)

Also, if you are pleased with our book then you can **Go to Amazon where you purchased this book and leave us a review!** In the world of an author who writes books independently, your reviews are not only touching but important so that we know you like the material we have prepared for "YOU" our audience! So, leave us a review...we would love to see that you enjoyed our book!

Table of Contents

Chapter 1:
The Electric Skillet Utility Book

It's A "One of a Kind" Instructional Book

There are many books that have been created for different types of recipes and even cookware. When you browse the magazine aisles at the supermarket or the cooking section at the local book store, you find quite a few books that are catered for grills, BBQs and slow cookers. However, this is the only book that has been written for the Electric Skillet.

Why Have a Book for this Electric Skillet?

Because it's one of a kind! This skillet is thee electric skillet of all electric skillets. Once you purchase it, you will learn that it is the only skillet that you will ever need. Every chapter in this book is perfectly crafted and laid out for this skillet. You will find everything that you need to know about this skillet in this book and by the time you are done, you will tell all your friends.

99 Ways to say "Yummmm!"

Every recipe in this book was handpicked for the Electric Skillet and its many uses. You will not find one recipe that you cannot use with this skillet, which is another way to show you why it is the best. From meats and pastas to breakfast and desserts, this Skillet Will Wow you. If you're strapped for time and need something to whip up in 20 minutes or less, or you're in the mood for steak and potatoes. You can create any of these fun filled and romantic dinners in the Electric Skillet, and much more.

Cook Like a Pro!

Learn Specific Cooking Recipes from This Electric Skillet That Make You Look Like a Pro! From beginners, to world-renowned chefs, The Electric Skillet is super easy to use, clean and even store. For those who are new to the world of cooking, This Electric Skillet should be your go to cookware of choice. You can make "one skillet meals" in here that will have your friends and family cheering and in no time, you can brush up on your cooking skills.

With the unique recipes that we have picked just for this electric skillet, you can become the type of cook that you want to be. This product is so versatile that you can learn to fry, roast and bake like any professional you've seen on TV and even one that would make your Grandmother proud.

It's the Healthiest Way to Cook to Lower Cholesterol

The greatest thing about The Electric Skillet is that it's Super Non-Stick. Unlike most other skillets or pans, a non-stick electric skillet does not require any fat or butter to keep food from sticking, flaking or breaking onto the skillet itself. Adding oils is not a must anymore but a choice...for flavor that is. This is important because all that butter and fat could cause a person to have very high cholesterol. This electric skillet is the healthier choice and helps lower your cholesterol one meal at a time.

"Toss Those Old Frying Pans..."
This Is the Only Non-Stick Skillet You'll Ever Need!

The Electric Skillet is virtually the only non-stick skillet that you will ever need. The non-stick cast aluminum is Teflon free and thus allows your food to slide off with ease, without the health risks that come with it. You can cook a variety of food on the skillet, even spaghetti, and do not have to worry if you need to put it in the oven to cook meals. This electric skillet is so versatile that you can heat it up to 400º F and even throw that "bad boy" in the dishwasher for a safe clean. However, if you want to go old fashioned, you can clean it off with a non-metal cleaning pad and store it safely next to other pans. Why wouldn't you want to add this great electric skillet to you or a loved one's cooking collection?

Chapter 2:
What's So Special About This
Electric Skillet?

Ultra-Durable, Energy Efficient, and Versatile

For this electric skillet, we have done our own unofficial analysis to put this thing to the test, but do not recommend you do the same. You know…shopping for an electric skillet can be a pretty important task. After all, you are going to be cooking all your food in this one skillet. So, you better make a good choice, right? There are so many kinds to choose from. How do you choose the best one for you? Well, for starters, you want an electric skillet that will last a long time. I know that I would be furious if I bought an electric skillet and had to throw it away within a couple of months because of scratches and the fact that the coating was starting to peel off. How unhealthy and unsanitary is that?

Well, I will be the first to tell you that this cast aluminum electric skillet is the best investment that you will ever make. Cast aluminum is a specific type of metal that can withstand high temperatures that are required to cook food, and it will remain useful for several years with minimal care It is also more energy efficient than using a common burner stove. The electric skillet can be used to roast, fry, grill, stew, and even bake. The other great thing about this electric skillet is that will never corrode or rust on you! "Now that's an electric skillet you want in your kitchen!"

"Do The Electric Slide!"

It's Like Cooking On Air… Food Slides Right Out of the Electric skillet! You have all your ingredients ready, but you are out of oil or butter, or you are trying to lose weight, but you need to coat your skillet with butter or oil so the food doesn't stick. What do you do? There is no need to worry because this cast aluminum electric skillet is Super Non-Stick. This means that the food you cook with it doesn't need any oil or butter. You can cook everything you need without it. It's that simple! You will actually feel like you are cooking on air because all of the food slides right out and onto the plate.

100% Safe: PFOA, PTFE and PFOS-Free

We are all aware of the danger of Teflon style non-stick skillets or pans. This is the brand that often gives non-stick pans a bad reputation because they can cause many different types of health issues. First of all, Teflon is a type of coating that is owned by the DuPont Company. Teflon coating is often fluoropolymer plastic (PTFE), Perfluoroctanoic Acid (PFOA) based. These chemicals are very harmful and can cause consumers to get very sick.

So, how can you tell if the electric skillet that you are looking for is safe? Well...this is one if the safest electric skillets you can buy on the market by my opinion! This Non-Stick Cast Aluminum Electric skillet does not contain these harmful chemicals! The lack of these chemicals make this product much safer for consumers and you can go about your cooking knowing that your health is safe!

SOAK IT!...It's Dishwasher Safe!

After a long day of cooking, the last thing anyone wants to do is clean up the kitchen. Thank God for your dishwasher, right? Wrong. Didn't you read that you couldn't put your non-stick skillet into the dishwasher and you had to refrain from certain soaps and other types of cleaners because they might ruin the surface of the electric skillet and cause it to erode? Well, you can scratch that. The Electric Skillet is dishwasher safe. Most non-stick skillets have a problem with dealing with high heats and this is the reason that you cannot put them in the dishwasher. This is not the case with the non-stick electric skillet. Being able to put it in the dishwasher leaves you with more time to do what you want and less time cleaning up the kitchen.

Chapter 3:
Non-Stick Cast Aluminum Benefits!

The Healthiest Choice in Cooking

We live in an age where people are starting to be more health conscious. We see this in everything that we do, from ads on TV to what we read in magazines. Why would our cookware be any different? This is where we cook the food that goes into our bodies. So, of this this is going to be important to us. Most of the food that we cook requires oils and butter so that it does not stick to the skillet.

Well, we no longer need to worry about that. This non-stick cast aluminum electric skillet requires no oils or butters. The non-stick coating that is on the base of the electric skillet keeps foods from sticking. That's the whole purpose of the non-stick aspect of this electric skillet, AND it is a major health benefit to us. Of course, we need some oils or fat to help the skin, this is where a little bit of olive or avocado oil can be used for some flavor. Just remember that this is not an essential ingredient for cooking anymore, rather a choice.

Turn That Heat Up!

This Electric Skillet Can Withstand High Levels of Heat up to 400º
You're cooking with your non-stick electric skillet and the recipe calls for putting the ingredients into the oven. So, what do you do? Do you transfer your ingredients to an oven safe dish? The answer is no. This cast aluminum non-stick skillet can withhold heat up to 400º F. So, you can basically use it like an oven. This is great. The whole dish isn't ruined and you don't have to worry about your electric skillet as well. These are things that all types of cook's care about; preserving the life of their cookware and saving the dish. After all, what is more important?

The Best All-Purpose of Cookware

Cast aluminum electric skillets are the top choice, as far as cookware durability and strength is concerned. Some of the great advantages of using this particular skillet is that it contains quick heating metal. This means that you cannot only use the skillet as a broiler or an oven, but that it is dishwasher safe as well. Since this skillet can heat up to high temperatures, it can serve as its own stove. This is another reason why many people tend to use this skillet for all their cooking needs.

Easy to Clean and Store

Taking proper care of your non-stick skillet is very important. This can ensure that you keep using this product for a very long time. One of the ways to do this is to keep your skillet clean for the best quality performance. Any food residue or leftover grease can actually cook onto the surface of the skillet, which can cause food to stick and defeat the whole purpose of a non-stick skillet. Leaving leftover food or residue on a non-stick skillet can be hard to remove later on. Just make sure that you wipe your skillet clean or wash it thoroughly every time.

It is also important to store your skillet properly to preserve its lifespan and performance. Do not store it inside other metal cookware because you do not want it to scratch. Store it on its own in a cabinet or other area where you store your personal cookware. This also gives the product room to breathe. I know this sounds funny, but even skillets need fresh air. Just remember, if you take care of your skillet, it will take care of you; your food that is.

Clean As a Whistle...But Not as Loud!

Staying healthy is a huge priority in the kitchen. This theme is universal when prepping/preparing and even cleaning up the food. And the theme stretches as far as what types of cookware that we are using. There are many arguments on why non-stick cast aluminum skillets are the best, but this reason is the icing on the cake. When cooking, there are many rules on how we are supposed to clean the surfaces, and cookware, as well as store them. Well, this particular skillet has one up on most of the other non-stick and stick electric skillets. **What is that? You say.**

You can submerge this electric skillet in water when cleaning it. It is a highly smart design that allows for this type of water submersion.

Chapter 4:
A History of the Non-Stick Skillet

Is the Non-Stick Skillet as Old
as the Ancient Greeks?

Non-stick cookware sounds like a new type of invention, right? Well, at least something that was created in the 19th or 20th century at least. The idea is over 2,000 years old. Due to an archaeology site found near Naples, archaeologists have determined that Romans used non-stick pans too. The problem of food sticking to pots must have frustrated them as well. Some of the pottery that was discovered was coated with a red, slippery coating that was determined to keep stews from sticking to the bottom of pots. How exciting is that?

The ancient Mycenaean's (Greeks) also used non-stick cookware to help preserve their bread. The Greeks used griddles to cook their bread and found that the dough was sticky and tended to burn onto the top of the griddles. There were two sides to the griddle, a smooth side and a side with holes. The bread was more than likely going to stick on the smooth surface of the griddle. However, the holes were actually an ancient non-stick secret. The holes ensured that the oil spread evenly over the surface of the griddle. So, now we know that Ancient Greeks and Romans were trying to find ways to cook better and easier.

DuPont's Discovery of Teflon

Did you know that Teflon was actually invented by accident? Roy Plunkett, a DuPont chemist, invented Teflon when he was trying to make a better refrigerator. The chemist decided to combine the gas form of tetrafluoroethylene with hydrochloric acid. When he gathered the gas, he pressurized and cooled it in canisters overnight. When he returned the next day, the gas was gone. Plunkett couldn't understand what happened. The gas weighed the same as they did the night before.

Plunkett decided to cut the canisters in half and noticed that the gas had hardened on all sides, creating a type of slick surface. Instead of throwing the canisters away, he and his assistant tested the new substance and found that it was extremely slippery, as well as inactive to all chemicals. This was an amazing find, but some of the best things are created by accident.

17

From Aerospace to Cookware

The creation of Teflon had nothing to do with cooking. That came about by accident as well. However, when Plunkett trademarked Teflon in 1945, it was picked up by the military and used as a type of artillery shell and in the construction of nuclear material for many projects, particularly the Manhattan Project.

Marc Gregoire, a French engineer who worked at a French aerospace research agency (ONERA) used Teflon to remove glass fiber molds. When his wife heard about this, she challenged him to create a type of nonstick cookware by adding Teflon to the base of aluminum pans. Thus, Teflon nonstick pans were made. A company known as Tefal decided to market this cooking invention and made it an international success. This invention has helped us find ways to cook the food in a much healthier way.

How Non-Stick Electric Skillets Are Made

If Non-Stick electric skillets are unique and special, shouldn't they be specially made? Well, they are. There is a specific chemical recipe that needs to be followed to ensure that the electric skillet is going to do what it was meant to do. Like keep things from sticking, which eliminates the use of butters and oils; essentially creating a healthier way for us to cook the food and watch the calorie intake.

The process starts with a ladle machine that creates a mold of melted aluminum, which makes the base of electric skillets. The excess is then cut off and the electric skillet is moved to a spot where a flame melts a series of powders onto the electric skillet to give it that coating that we have grown to know and love. When referring to the cast aluminum electric skillet for the newer style skillets...there is another process involved but these are the basics of the non-stick electric skillet and how they are made and have come into existence! **"Things that make you go...Hmmmmmm..."**

Chapter 5:
Using Your Nonstick
Cast Aluminum Electric Skillet

This Non-Stick Electric Skillet Will
Transform Your Cooking

Tired of your same old pots, pans, and skillets? Tired of the scrubbing, the scratches and the coating that comes off and changes the taste of your food and ends up in your mouth? Well, this non-stick skillet will transform your cooking. For starters, those who have a busy schedule can use it to create dishes they never thought possible, in the same skillet and in under 30 minutes.

However, with all the recipes that we provide in this book, you can grow from just a beginner to the person Grandma is calling to bring dessert to the next family holiday or get together. This skillet is every cooks dream because it is so easy to use and it takes all the worry out of cooking. Before you know it, you will be dying to get into the kitchen and cook all those healthy meals that you never dreamed of making before.

It's Easy...But Not Greasy!

The whole reason behind the creation of non-stick skillets was to make cooking easier and healthier. No one likes their food sticking to the cookware, and who wants to use all that oil and butter? We all know that it's tradition to throw in a teaspoon of butter or oil to the pan and let it melt before cooking, but sometimes it's okay to break away from that tradition and create your own. With this non-stick electric skillet, you can make your own tradition and start cooking without butter or oils, unless you choose to use them for flavor. Believe me; your health will thank us.

Using Your Electric Skillet

When using new cookware, it is imperative that we know what we are doing. This ensures that we not only make good food, but that we protect ourselves and our cookware as well. The first thing that we should do is know how to put the electric skillet together. When assembling, the electric skillet place the skillet, itself, upside down on any surface. There will be four screws attached to the mounting projections on the skillet body; remove those. Next, place the handle on the skillet, by lining up the holes in the handles with the mounting projections, and refasten the screws, strong and securely.

Now that the skillet is secure, we can talk about how to use it. First things first, or should I say second? Before we use our electric skillet for the first time, it is important that you wash it, and cover in warm water, rinse and dry; or you can choose to put it in the dishwasher, just remember to not put the Control Master heat control anywhere near the water. You can choose to season your skillet by lightly rubbing oil on its surface. Remove any overflow cooking oil with a towel.

Next, you are going to place the skillet on a dry surface that can withstand heat. Insert the Control Master control into the skillet, and plug the cord into an outlet. Now, you can turn the electric skillet on to the temperature that you need. Just remember to remove the cover when you are preheating the skillet. The pilot light will turn off when it reaches the designated temperature.

When you are preparing your food, remember that you do not have to use any oil if you do not want to. Place your food into the skillet and cook according to the temperature table (provided below). You can adjust the heat according to your preference. Turn off the heat when cooking is completed, unplug from wall, and allow for it to cool down before cleaning.

There are some safety tips that you need to know. This electric skillet is not made for deep frying foods. Do not use outdoors. Please do not place near a stove or a heated oven, and make sure that the cord does not touch any hot surfaces.

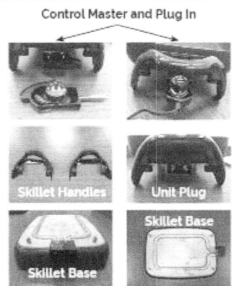

Temperature Chart of Greatness!

Baking	Temperature	Cooking Time
Pancakes	350-400 degrees	2-3 minutes
Frying	**Temperature**	**Cooking Time**
Bacon	300-325 degrees	8-10 minutes
Canadian bacon	275-300 degrees	3-4 minutes
Chicken	325-350 degrees	25-40 minutes
Eggs, fried	250-275 degrees	3-5 minutes
Eggs, scrambled	250-275 degrees	3-5 minutes
Fish	325-375 degrees	5-10 minutes
French Toast	300-325 degrees	4-6 minutes
Ham ½ thick	325-350 degrees	10-12 minutes
Ham ¾ thick	325-350 degrees	14-16 minutes
Hamburgers	325-375 degrees	8-12 minutes
Minute Steak	375-400 degrees	4-5 minutes
Pork Chops ½ thick	325-375 degrees	15-20 minutes
Pork Chops ¾ thick	325-375 degrees	20-25 minutes
Potatoes	300-350 degrees	10-12 minutes
Sausage, link	300-325 degrees	20-30 minutes
Sausage, precooked	325-350 degrees	10-12 minutes
Sandwiches, grilled	300-325 degrees	5-10 minutes
Steak, rare	350-400 degrees	6-7 minutes
Steak, medium	350-400 degrees	10-12 minutes

Broiling – When you want your food to reach the temperature just below the boiling point, you will preheat the skillet at 350 degrees. Once your food starts to boil, put on the cover and then start simmering. In order to keep the food at this particular temperature, keep the temperature between warm and 200 degrees. Foods will reach this point between the settings of warm and 200 degrees.

Pressure Cook – What better way to braise or roast your meat then putting it in the pressure cooker? All this means is that you want to brown your meat or vegetable. In order to use, keep the skillet at the temperatures between 325-350 degrees.

Keep Warm – When you want to keep your food warm after cooking, just turn the temperature to warm. It's that easy!

Chapter 6:
Learn from the Pros!...Pro Tips

Mom Says..."Marinate That Meats!"

You often think of marinating your steak or chicken breast during barbeque season. What if I told you that marinating your meat was good for your health? Well, it is. Marinating your beef, poultry and fish can help decrease the carcinogenic heterocyclic amines (HCAs) that are produced when meat is grilled or cooked at high temperature levels. Marinating the meat first can reduced these levels by 99 percent, and if you add a touch of rosemary to the marinade that you make, it could help decrease this even more.

There are a few more reasons why using marinates can be beneficial to your meats prior to cooking. For instance, the acidic quality within the marinade can help slow down bacteria growth (when using citrus juices and vinegars.) But remember to always keep your meats soaking with your marinated in the fridge where your meats will stay cool and safe. Another great thing about marinates, besides the flavor, is that the juices can also tenderize the meat for you. This will help with digestion, so that the meat goes down smoothly. Lastly, marinates help keep the meat moist. So, you will never have to hear your mother-in-law tell you that your meat is dry and tough.
...And that's one to grow on!

Cooking with Meats that have Fats...

Is This a Substitute for Oil and Butter? Well...this is really a topic to talk about! If you are cooking with oils and butter, and also have fats on the meat that you are cooking with...you are just adding more oils to the cooking process. This will increase the fat content of your foods tremendously, and this is what you will be eating as a result of that! If there are recipes that call for oils or butter...check to see how much fat is on the meat. I know that you cannot calculate this precisely, but if you are aware that the meat you are cooking with has fat on it then you can scale back the amount of oil (or butter) that you are cooking with. This only makes sense because the recipe does not know how much fat is on your meat anyway. The fat content on meats will not only be a fat substitute, but it will also be something that flavors your foods in the process! If you cut down the amount of oil, grease and butter that you are cooking with you will be eating and serving much healthier recipes, keeping your cholesterol levels lower from not using that additional oil in your foods.

Now…That's One to Grow On! :)

Know Your Fats and Oils:

"Cooking and Cholesterol" There is something to say about vegetable oils. They are the most "all-purpose oils" and probably the least expensive types of oils to cook with. There are oils that you may not have noticed or considered as an alternative to cook with, and here are just a few to keep in mind. Almond oil, Coconut Oil, Grape seed Oil and Avocado Oils, just to name a few for a little range of variation and diversity.

There are other oils that are great for foods but you may think about the heat exposure because these oils burn very easily when exposed to high cooking temperatures. These oils are normally utilized best when added to a salad or even a nice pasta dish or even best on vegetables for that added flavor! Such oils consist of oils that come from different types of nuts, sesame oil and we don't want to forget that extra virgin olive oil!

One oil that is extremely popular and not as expensive as the ones that were just mentioned is an "All Favorite" The Regular Olive Oil! This type of oil is a great cooking oil and adds a good flavor to your foods as well but just keep in mind again about the temperature that you are cooking with because this is one that can burn at high temperatures as well!

Just read the labels to see which different flavors will go best with the foods you are cooking, and keep in mind the amount of heat that the oils can withstand…"
And That's Another One to Grow On!"

Garnishing with Parsley:
It's More Than Just for Decoration!

We are all familiar with the green leafed tree that decorates the plates at restaurants. Did you know that parsley was actually more than a garnish? This herb is a jack of all trades in the culinary world, and should be treated as such. First of all, the herb is packed with Vitamin A, B, C, E, K, and it's great for your digestion. No wonder chefs have been putting it on your plate for years. It is supposed to be eaten after your meal. However, parsley can be used to eliminate waste, maintain gas, and relieves bloating, water retention and does this with its anti-inflammatory substances. This little green garnish can even help freshens your breath.

So, grab a leaf and bon a petite.

Parsley should be called the next Superfood. Not only is it packet with a ton of vitamins, but it can be used as an antibiotic and may aid against other bodily illnesses or infections as well. As an antibiotic, parsley boosts the immune system and may also help prevent other things like the common cold or flu, as well as treat bladder and urinary tract infections. The herb also contains high amounts of apigenin, which is an anticancer property. Eating parsley may help reduce the risk of beast, skin, prostrate and other cancers. The herb can also be used as an anti-inflammatory, as well as a detoxifier; eating it will definitely help keep you healthy. So, the next time a chef adorns your plate with a leaf of parsley, you should thank her for caring about your health enough to put it on your plate.

Chapter 7:
When the Food's Done...Put it Up!

Have you ever cleaned out your fridge and noticed all of the food that was sitting in your garbage can? Throwing food away can be very expensive and believe me, no one likes throwing money into the trash. This is one of the reasons why knowing the right ways to preserving your food is so important. This chapter will provide tips on how to store your food to avoid foodborne illnesses, preserve its shelf life and even save money.

Store All Leftovers in Airtight,
Leak-proof Containers

Food safety is important when it comes to protecting the health. One of the best ways to do this is to store all of your leftovers from tonight's meal in air-tight, leak-proof containers. These containers protect against air-borne bacteria, pests and even leaks. When used correctly, they will protect the shelf life, taste and longevity of your leftovers. Now you and your family can continue to enjoy them for a little bit longer.

Glass containers with snap on lids are the best containers to use when storing food. Plastic containers can stain when storing food, such as spaghetti sauce or enchiladas. Glass containers do not stain as easily. Also, when storing food in plastic containers it is hard to see what is actually inside them. Storing food in glass containers help you see what is inside. Remember to label the date that you cooked and stored the food. This will give you a good idea of how old it is and when you need to dispose of it.

Separate Leftovers in Small Containers to Cool Faster

There is a myth about storing hot or warm food in the fridge right away. Many people say that when you place large amounts of hot food into the fridge before cooling it down, it can cause the temperature to rise in the fridge, which can warm up all of the other food inside as well. So, the hot food will not only cool down rapidly, but it will warm up everything else. Even if this is the case, refrigerators were invented to keep food cool and not be affected by the warmth of newly cooked food. It is far more dangerous to let food sit out at room temperature to cool then to place it in the fridge while it is still warm.

When cooking large amounts of food, like stews, it can be easier to separate the leftovers into small containers. This can be beneficial for two reasons. First, it will allow the food to cool down much faster and at a safer temperature. Putting the food in more than one container lets it cool down without the risk of spoiling outside of the container or making the other food in the fridge warmer. Secondly, it becomes convenient for reheating small amounts for lunch or an individual dinner at home. Reheating the food in the microwave more than once can cause problems as well. So, this eliminates the problem of warming up more than you can eat at one time.

Refrigerate Leftover Foods Within Two Hours of Cooking and Cooling

Refrigerating or freezing leftovers to preserve them is important. It is not only a healthy tip, but a financial one as well. In order to make sure that we and the families are eating healthy food, we need to make sure that we are preserving it correctly. Bacteria grows at a fast rate between the 40° F and 140° F range. Hot food must be kept at 140° F or higher to prevent bacteria. Food must be refrigerated at 41° F or lower to prevent everyone from getting sick.

Store your leftovers within two hours of cooking food and within one hour, if the temperature in the room is over 90 degrees. It is very important to adhere to these safety tips because it can be harmful to your health or that of your family if you don't. These tips can help keep you from getting sick from the bacteria that lingers around improperly handled food.

Divide Your Meats for a Longer
and Safer Shelf Life

Just like fruits and vegetables, separating leftover meat is important to maintaining a longer shelf life. Cooling the meat and putting them in shallow or separate containers keeps it fresh longer. Divide the large portions into smaller quantities. If the food cooked in a very hot container, then you want to put it into a container that doesn't keep it from cooling. One thing also to remember is not to pack the food tightly in the container or the refrigerator. Keeping a proper airflow helps maintain the temperature in the meat and helps it cool off. This way it will last longer and will be easy to grab when you want a good snack.

Chapter 8:
The "Electric" Menu!

When reading these recipes just remember that you are reading the views and opinions of the writer. We have also provided the nutritional values on all of these recipes "for all of your calorie counters out there." So...Turn the page and "Dive - Head First" and get cooking! :)

Chapter 9:
BEEF:

Where's the beef you might ask, it's right here in this chapter! All the tasty, mouthwatering, succulent, luscious, tender, rich, heavenly, divine, juicy and yummy beef recipes right here at your fingertips! Yes, my friend's...beef is on the menu!

SHREDDED CABBAGE RICE ROLLS

Take a modern-day twist on a classic. Cabbage rolls usually take a lot of preparation time with stuffing whole cabbage leaves. With this recipe, you can save on time without compromising on the flavors that you love.

Prep Time: 10 Minutes
Cook Time: 35 Minutes
Servings: 4

INGREDIENTS

1 1/2 lbs. lean ground beef
1 small onion diced
1/2 shredded medium head of cabbage
1 can 14.5 oz. stewed tomatoes
1 can 14.5 oz. diced tomatoes
1 can tomato sauce

1 tsp. sugar,
3 tsp. cider vinegar
3/4 cup water
3/4 cup long-grain white rice
Sea salt
Pepper

DIRECTIONS

〉 Cook ground beef for 5 minutes on high heat.
〉 Add the diced onions, cabbage, tomatoes, tomato sauce, sugar and vinegar with the ground beef and continue cooking for 4 minutes or until ground beef is browned.
〉 Add the water and rice to the skillet and simmer for 25 minutes, adding cheese, salt and pepper as desired.

NUTRITIONAL FACTS:

Serving Size 1 Serving, Calories 562, Calories from Fat 105, Total Fat 11.7g, Saturated Fat 4.2g, Cholesterol 152mg, Sodium 1165mg, Potassium 1891mg, Carbohydrates 54.6g, Dietary Fiber 9.4g, Sugars 17.3g, Protein 59.8g

Vitamin A 45% · Vitamin C 170%, Calcium 13% · Iron 201%, Based on a 2000 calorie diet

NUTRITIONAL ANALYSIS / GOOD POINTS:

Very high in iron, High in phosphorus, High in selenium, Very high in vitamin B6, Very high in vitamin B12, Very high in vitamin C, High in zinc

MINCED MEATBALL GARLIC SPAGHETTI

This recipe has all of the makings of a classic family recipe, but without all of the work. Here you can throw your uncooked noodles and cook them in the same spot as the sauce. So, put yourself a glass of wine and enjoy this easy One Electric Skillet Spaghetti.

Prep Time: 35 Minutes
Cook Time: 35 Minutes
Servings: 4

INGREDIENTS

24 oz. pasta sauce (1 jar)
1 cup water
24 meatballs (fresh or precooked)
16 oz. pasta, (broken in half)

1 cup mozzarella cheese (shredded part-skim)
½ cup parmesan cheese (grated)

DIRECTIONS

> Put the spaghetti sauce, meatballs and the noodles in to a non-stick electric skillet until it boils.
> Cover the electric skillet, and simmer for 25 minutes. Remember to stir the noodles to keep from sticking.
> When done, top with cheese and serve.

NUTRITIONAL FACTS:

Serving Size 903 g, Amount per Serving, Calories 1,666, Calories from Fat 813, Total Fat 90.3g, Saturated Fat 35.6g, Trans Fat 0.0g, Cholesterol 331mg, Sodium 3562mg, Potassium 741mg, Total Carbohydrates 123.5g, Dietary Fiber 10.4g, Sugars 21.0g, Protein 123.0g

Vitamin A 25%, Vitamin C 6%, Calcium 51%, Iron 28%, Nutrition Grade C-, Based on a 2000 calorie diet

I LOVE STEAK AND POTATOES SKILLET

Steak and potatoes in only 30 minutes. This recipe is paired with frozen potatoes and frozen veggies that give you a full balanced meal in under an amazing meal you will devour.

Prep Time: 30 Minutes
Cook Time: 30 Minutes
Servings: 4

INGREDIENTS

1 lb. boneless beef sirloin steak, cut into 4 serving pieces
¾ tsp. seasoned salt
½ tsp. garlic-pepper blend
1 ½ cups frozen stir-fry vegetables

1 bag refrigerated home-style potato slices
4 oz. or 1/2 cup shredded American-Cheddar cheese blend

DIRECTIONS -

> Place the steak into a non-stick electric skillet and sprinkle with the seasoned salt and garlic pepper.
> Cook on medium heat for 2 minutes on each side.
> Remove steak from skillet and add vegetables, cooking for 2 minutes.
> Put in potatoes and cook for 10 minutes.
> When done, put in the steak and mix together before serving.

NUTRITIONAL FACTS:

Serving Size 407 g, Amount Per Serving, Calories 513, Calories from Fat 150, Total Fat 16.7g, Saturated Fat 8.7g, Cholesterol 131mg, Sodium 554mg, Potassium 1518mg, Total Carbohydrates 42.6g, Dietary Fiber 6.1g, Sugars 2.9g, Protein 46.6g

Vitamin A 28%, Vitamin C 87%, Calcium 23%, Iron 132%, Nutrition Grade A-, Based on a 2000 calorie diet

NUTRITIONAL ANALYSIS / GOOD POINTS

Low in sugar, Very high in iron, High in phosphorus, High in selenium, Very high in vitamin B6, Very high in vitamin B12, High in vitamin C, High in zinc

NEW DELI INDIAN CURRY SKILLET

DESCRIPTION

Indian meets Chinese. This dish will have you adding ground beef to a curry and then throwing it over rice. What it won't have you do is dislike the flavor.

Prep Time: 50 Minutes
Cook Time: 50 Minutes
Servings: 6

INGREDIENTS

1 ½ cups uncooked white rice
1 lb. lean ground beef
1 small chopped onion, chopped (1/4 cup)
1 chopped clove garlic
2 tsp. gingerroot (grated)
1 tsp. tomato paste

1 tsp. Salt
2 tsp. ground cumin
2 tsp. chili powder
1 tsp. Garam masala
29 oz. diced tomatoes (2 cans)
3 tsp. chopped fresh cilantro

DIRECTIONS -

> Put beef, onion, garlic and gingerroot into non-stick electric skillet and cook for 7 minutes.
> Add the rest of the ingredients and simmer uncovered for 10 minutes.
> Put over the cooked rice, add cilantro and serve.

NUTRITIONAL FACTS:

Serving Size 276 g, Amount Per Serving, Calories 348, Calories from Fat 51, Total Fat 5.7g, Saturated Fat 2.0g, Cholesterol 68mg, Sodium 459mg19%, Potassium 749mg, Total Carbohydrates 45.0g, Dietary Fiber 3.0g, Sugars 4.4g, Protein 27.9g,

Vitamin A 29%, Vitamin C 34%, Calcium 4%, Iron 96%, Nutrition Grade A, Based on a 2000 calorie diet

NUTRITIONAL ANALYSIS / GOOD POINTS

Very high in iron, High in selenium, Very high in vitamin B6, Very high in vitamin B12, High in zinc

NO MAS TORTILLA BURRITOS

One of my favorite and, most fun to make! If you're ever in doubt…Burritos are on the menu! A nice big chunk of "Mouth Watering Mexican Flavored Bliss" is about to happen for dinner. Dive in and taste this Mexican goodness!

DESCRIPTION

Want all the taste of a burrito but don't want the carbs. This one stop no tortilla Ground Beef Burritos has all the makings of a great dish, but throw out the tortilla. You won't even miss it.

Prep Time: 30 Minutes
Cook Time: 30 Minutes
Servings: 4

INGREDIENTS

1 lb. lean ground beef
1 pkg. Taco Seasoning Mix
16 oz. can red kidney beans
1 cup Thick & Chunky Salsa

1 cup water
1 cup Mexican Style Shredded Cheese
1/3 cup the cream
1 large chopped green onion

DIRECTIONS

> Add all ingredients to a non-stick skillet and bring to a boil for 5 minutes.
> When cooled off, add the cream, onions and serve.

NUTRITIONAL FACTS:

Serving Size 414 g, Amount Per Serving, Calories 511, Calories from Fat 193, Total Fat 21.5g, Saturated Fat 11.3g, Trans Fat 0.0g, Cholesterol 139mg, Sodium 1491mg, Potassium 998mg, Total Carbohydrates 28.6g, Dietary Fiber 6.4g, Sugars 2.6g, Protein 48.7g

Vitamin A 17%, Vitamin C 6%, Calcium 30%, Iron 131%, Nutrition Grade B+, Based on a 2000 calorie diet

NUTRITIONAL ANALYSIS / GOOD POINTS

Low in sugar, Very high in iron
High in phosphorus, High in selenium, Very high in vitamin B6, Very high in vitamin B12
High in zinc

SIZZLING SOUTHWEST SHERRY FILET MIGNON

Who doesn't love steak and onions? Top with sweet sherry and a toasted French baguette and you will have a meal that will make your mouth water for more. – Just wrote this one. Was not on the original.

Prep Time: 45 Minutes
Cook Time: 45 Minutes
Servings: 4

INGREDIENTS

1 lb. filet mignon (trimmed and cut into 4 steaks)
1/2 tsp. minced dried onion
1/2 tsp. salt
1/2 tsp. freshly ground pepper
2 large chopped sweet onions
1/3 cup dry sherry wine

1 tsp. all-purpose flour
1 cup beef broth
2 tsp. fresh chopped thyme
4 slices baguettes (toasted whole-grain)
1/2 cup shredded Swiss cheese

DIRECTIONS

> Season the steaks with onion, salt and pepper and add them to a non-stick skillet.
> Cook for 3 minutes on each side.
> Remove the steaks and add the add the onions and sherry to the skillet.
> Cover and cook on high for 8 minutes
> Put the flour, broth, thyme and bring to a small boil.
> Add the steaks back to the skillet and top with a slice of baguette and cheese
> Place in the oven and cook for 2 minutes.
> Serve

NUTRITIONAL FACTS:

Serving Size 316 g, Amount Per Serving, Calories 407, Calories from Fat 111,, Total Fat 12.3g, Saturated Fat 5.5g, Cholesterol 87mg, Sodium 787mg33%, Potassium 659mg, Total Carbohydrates 27.6g, Dietary Fiber 2.7g, Sugars 4.5g, Protein 41.4g

Vitamin A 3%, Vitamin C 9%, Calcium 18%, Iron 24%, Nutrition Grade C+, Based on a 2000 calorie diet

NUTRITIONAL ANALYSIS / GOOD POINTS

High in niacin, High in phosphorus, Very high in selenium, High in vitamin B6, High in zinc

GARLIC AND MUSHROOM GROUND BEEF STROGANOF

My mother used to make this dish with pieces of stew meat and would place it over rice. Here is a nice take on the dish with your own flare. Show your mom that you can share her up in the kitchen and do it in style.

Prep Time: 20 Minutes
Cook Time: 35 Minutes
Servings: 4

INGREDIENTS

1 lb. ground beef
1 chopped onion
1 tsp. garlic powder
1/4 tsp. black pepper
1/2 pound chopped fresh mushrooms

1 can condensed cream of mushroom soup
1 1/2 cups the cream
1/2-pound cooked egg noodles

DIRECTIONS -

- Add the onion and ground beef into a non-stick skillet and cook until meat is brown.
- -Put in garlic powder, and mushrooms. Cook for 3 minutes.
- -Put in the soup and simmer for 10 minutes.
- -Serve over rice or noodles and add the cream to the mixture.

NUTRITIONAL FACTS

Serving Size 418 g, Amount Per Serving, Calories 564, Calories from Fat 279, Total Fat 31.0g48%, Saturated Fat 15.2g76%, Trans Fat 0.0g, Cholesterol 156mg52%, Sodium 620mg26%, Potassium 880mg25%, Total Carbohydrates 28.1g9%, Dietary Fiber 1.9g8%, Sugars 3.8g, Protein 43.1g

Vitamin A 12%, Vitamin C 7%, Calcium 12%, Iron 135%, Nutrition Grade B, Based on a 2000 calorie diet

NUTRITIONAL ANALYSIS / GOOD POINTS

Low in sugar, Very high in iron, High in selenium, Very high in vitamin B6, Very high in vitamin B12

BIG TEXAS BEAN AND BACON BURGERS

Cooked in a skillet and not over the BBQ. This Kicking Bacon Burger dish still packs a punch and is very easy to make.

Prep Time: 5 Minutes
Cook Time: 15 Minutes
Servings: 6

INGREDIENTS

1 1/2 lbs. ground beef
1 can Condensed Bean with Bacon Soup
1/2 cup water

1 tsp. horseradish
6 slices yellow Cheddar cheese
6 Sesame Topped Hamburger Buns

DIRECTIONS -

- Create 6 burgers from the ground beef.
- Add the burgers in a non-stick electric skillet and cook for 10 minutes.
- Put in the soup, water and horseradish and bring to a boil.
- Cover and cook for 5 minutes.
- Add the cheese and cook until melted.
- Serve on the buns.

NUTRITIONAL FACTS:

Serving Size 210 g, Amount Per Serving, Calories 422, Calories from Fat 151, Total Fat 16.8g, Saturated Fat 7.6g, Trans Fat 0.0g, Cholesterol 127mg, Sodium 667mg, Potassium 608mg, Total Carbohydrates 21.1g, Dietary Fiber 1.1g, Sugars 4.6g, Protein 44.1g

Vitamin A 6%, Vitamin C 3%, Calcium 22%, Iron 127%, Nutrition Grade B, Based on a 2000 calorie diet

NUTRITIONAL ANALYSIS / GOOD POINTS

Very high in iron, High in phosphorus, High in selenium, Very high in vitamin B6, Very high in vitamin B12, High in zinc

TENDER TERIYAKI BRAISED BEEF & BROCCOLI

Nothing is simpler than cooking everything in the same pot, and an added bonus is when it doesn't take a long time. Rice, vegetables, and beef make this entrée an entire meal in one, and the teriyaki sauce provides a flavorful theme to the dish. Just toss in, stir, and dinner will be ready in no time!

Prep Time: 10 Minutes
Cook Time: 15 Minutes
Servings: 5

INGREDIENTS

1 lb. lean ground beef (at least 80%)
12 oz. frozen chopped broccoli (1 bag)
1/2 cup chopped green onions (1 Bunch - separate white and green parts)

1/2 Cup of chopped shallots
3 cups cold cooked white rice
1 cup marinade (thick teriyaki sauce)

DIRECTIONS

> Cook beef over medium-high heat, stirring frequently, until brown adding with salt to taste...keep the juice.
> Also cook broccoli as directed.
> Stir in green onions and shallots to electric skillet with beef, and cook for about a minute or so.
> Add rice and teriyaki sauce and stir as it cooks, just for a couple of minutes...till rice is cooked.
> Last add broccoli and green onions...stir for about 30 seconds. Done!

NUTRITIONAL FACTS:

Serving Size 344 g, Amount Per Serving, Calories 676, Calories from Fat 89, Total Fat 9.9g, Saturated Fat 2.4g, Trans Fat 0.0g, Cholesterol 81mg, Sodium 1281mg, Potassium 774mg, Total Carbohydrates 106.6g, Dietary Fiber 4.0g, Sugars 7.7g, Protein 37.7g

Vitamin A 27%, Vitamin C 85%, Calcium 7%, Iron 126%, Nutrition Grade A, Based on a 2000 calorie diet

NUTRITIONAL ANALYSIS / GOOD POINTS

Low in saturated fat, High in iron, High in selenium, Very high in vitamin B6, Very high in vitamin B12, High in vitamin C

JUICY MARINATED DIJON QUARTER LOIN

Flank steak is a great and versatile meat to marinade, especially if the sauce is extraordinarily tasty. You cannot go wrong with red wine vinegar, Dijon mustard, and lemon in anything, but imagine all mixed together with Worcestershire sauce, garlic, and black pepper! Don't forget to marinade for a long time, preferably 6 hours and get ready to wipe the water from your mouth afterwards.

Prep Time: 15 Minutes
Cook Time: 10 Minutes
Servings: 4

INGREDIENTS

1/2 cup vegetable oil
1/4 cup red wine vinegar
2 tablespoons fresh lemon juice
2 tablespoons Worcestershire sauce
1 tablespoon Dijon mustard

2 cloves garlic, minced
1/2 teaspoon ground black pepper
1/2 teaspoon onion powder
1/2 teaspoon sea salt
1 1/2 pounds flank steak

DIRECTIONS

⟩ In a medium sized container, mix the vinegar with the oil. Add lemon juice, Worcestershire sauce, mustard, garlic, onion powder, salt and ground black pepper. Place meat in dish and soak the steak with the marinade by putting it all over, coating generously. Cover...put in refrigerate for 5-6 hours.

⟩ Turn on the griddle for medium-high heat and add oil..

⟩ Add steaks to the skillet. (you are done with the marinade.) Cook meat on the skillet. About 6 minutes per side or to your liking.

NUTRITIONAL FACTS:

Serving Size 234 g, Amount Per Serving, Calories 590, Calories from Fat 375, Total Fat 41.6g, Saturated Fat 11.3g, Trans Fat 0.0g, Cholesterol 94mg, Sodium 459mg, Potassium 613mg, Total Carbohydrates 2.9g, Sugars 1.9g, Protein 47.7g

Vitamin A 0%, Vitamin C 7%, Calcium 3%, Iron 19%, Nutrition Grade C+, Based on a 2000 calorie diet

NUTRITIONAL ANALYSIS / GOOD POINTS

Low in sugar. High in niacin, High in selenium

SUCCULENT ELECTRIC SKILLET-SEARED GARLIC TENDERLOIN

There are not many more basic main courses than a juicy piece of steak. The great thing about straightforward meals is that they are fast, and with the right piece of meat, they are delicious. We will keep it simple: steak, salt, and pepper. If it ain't broke, don't fix it as the saying goes!

Prep Time: 15 Minutes
Cook Time: 15 Minutes
Servings: 2

INGREDIENTS

12 oz. steaks (can use 2 6oz flat iron tenderloin)
1 Tbsp. olive oil
1/2 teaspoon garlic powder
1/2 teaspoon onion powder
1/2 teaspoon black pepper
1 pinch of salt (to taste)

DIRECTIONS

> After bringing steak to room temperature, pat the meat with a paper towel to remove moisture. Season with the salt and pepper and onion and garlic powders.
> Add oil to your electric skillet while heating electric skillet.
> Let the steaks cook for a few minutes turning them over and repeating after first side is cooked, then flip and cook for another 3 minutes. Turn over the steaks and cook for another 2 to 3 minutes. Check steaks to see if they are cooked to your liking, but each side should be at least a golden brown.
> Slice and serve the steak after letting it cool for several minutes.

NUTRITIONAL FACTS:

Serving Size 180 g, Amount Per Serving, Calories 404, Calories from Fat 140, Total Fat 15.5g, Saturated Fat 3.9g, Cholesterol 153mg, Sodium 155mg, Potassium 588mg, Total Carbohydrates 1.3g, Protein 61.7g Vitamin A 0%, Vitamin C 1%, Calcium 1%, Iron 32%, Nutrition Grade B, Based on a 2000 calorie diet

NUTRITIONAL ANALYSIS / GOOD POINTS

Low in sodium, Very low in sugar, Very high in selenium, High in vitamin B12, High in zinc

THICK STACKED SIZZLING BURGERS ON THE STOVETOP

Burgers: American as apple pie, which should remind you not to forget dessert. However, many grill their burgers without realizing they can quickly be cooked on the stovetop using a griddle or skillet. With the right meat and the proper technique, the family can have burgers year round, but try not to get addicted!

Prep Time: 10 Minutes
Cook Time: 10 Minutes (or less)
Servings: 6

INGREDIENTS

1 1/2 pounds ground beef, 80% to 85% lean
9.5 oz. hamburger buns (6 Buns)
1/4 Stick butter (use oil as substitute if desired)
Pinch Salt
Pinch fresh black pepper
6 slices cheese

Burger toppings:
2 sliced tomatoes,
1/4 Onion (sliced)
2 pickles
3 tbsp. ketchup
2 tbsp. mustard
6 lettuce leaves

DIRECTIONS

> Shape the ground beef into 6 big and chunky patties.
> Melt butter on an electric skillet over medium heat.
> Lightly butter the buns, then toasting them to your desired liking. Move the buns to a clean plate.
> Using the same electric skillet, Cook the patties for several minutes. Add a pinch of salt and pepper to each and continue to cook for 3 to 4 minutes.
> Flip the burgers and repeat the process, adding a little more salt and pepper than before. Cook for another several minutes or until cooked to your desired liking.

NUTRITIONAL FACTS:

Serving Size 412 g, Amount Per Serving, Calories 779, Calories from Fat 315, Total Fat 35.0g, Saturated Fat 17.3g, Cholesterol 211mg, Sodium 1297mg, Potassium 1047mg, Total Carbohydrates 42.6g, Dietary Fiber 3.6g, Sugars 9.7g, Protein 70.9g

Vitamin A 26%, Vitamin C 19%, Calcium 44%, Iron 198%, Nutrition Grade B, Based on a 2000 calorie diet

NUTRITIONAL ANALYSIS / GOOD POINTS

Very high in iron, High in selenium, Very high in vitamin B6, Very high in vitamin B12, High in zinc

Chapter 10:
POULTRY:

In this section...chicken is on the menu! When preparing these gourmet poultry pounders...your friends will think you went to culinary school for years or married a professional chef for all the wrong reasons. All of these authentic menu item will have you running to the hen house to re-stock your refrigerator with these mouthwatering marinated delicacies! This section will be the best thing that has happened to you in a long time...All you have to do is pick a chick!

ZESTY BASIL CRUSTED CHICKEN

This low in calories and carbohydrates chicken and vegetables dish is not only easy to cook but it is really tasty. You won't believe that it's good for you because of its amazing, mouthwatering, lip-smacking taste.

Prep Time: 5 Minutes
Cook Time: 35 Minutes
Se**rvings:** 3

INGREDIENTS

Salt and pepper for taste
1 pound boneless, skinless chicken meat, cut into bite-sized pieces
1 red bell pepper, washed and diced
8 ounces mushrooms, cleaned and sliced

2 cups zucchini or other summer squash (washed, stemmed and sliced)
3 garlic cloves (minced or pressed)
8 ounces fresh basil (chopped)

DIRECTIONS

> Season the chicken with salt and pepper for taste.
> Add the chicken to a non-stick skillet, cooking on both sides until brown.
> Put in the rest of the ingredients and cook for 3 minutes.
> Serve

NUTRITIONAL FACTS:

Serving Size 420 g, Amount Per Serving, Calories 350Calories from Fat 110, Total Fat 12.2g, Saturated Fat 3.1g, Cholesterol 135mg, Sodium 147mg, Potassium 1124mg, Total Carbohydrates 10.4g, Dietary Fiber 3.7g15%, Sugars 4.5g, Protein 50.0g

Vitamin A 109%, Vitamin C 134%, Calcium 18%, Iron 38%, Nutrition Grade A, Based on a 2000 calorie diet

NUTRITIONAL ANALYSIS / GOOD POINTS

Low in sodium, High in iron, High in manganese, Very high in niacin, High in phosphorus, High in riboflavin, High in selenium, Very high in vitamin A, Very high in vitamin B6, Very high in vitamin C

GRILLED COWBOY CORNBREAD CHICKEN

Chicken and cornbread is a staple in any American household and is something that you can never get enough of. This recipe will bring you back to the western days and you will love the taste of BBQ chicken cooked right into the buttery cornbread.

Prep Time: 5 Minutes
Cook Time: 45 Minutes
Servings: 6

INGREDIENTS

8.5 oz. corn muffin mix (1 box)
½ cup the cream
2 tbsp. butter, melted
1 egg
½ cups corn kernels
1 diced red onion
Kosher salt
Freshly ground black pepper

2 cups shredded chicken (rotisserie best)
1 1/3 cup BBQ sauce
1 oz. lime juice
1 cup shredded cheddar
8oz gouda cheese (shredded)
¼ cup diced scallions

DIRECTIONS

> Bake the corn muffin mix, the cream, butter, egg and corn in a non-stick electric skillet for 20 minutes on 400 degrees.
> In another non-stick electric skillet cook onions and chicken until chicken is fully cooked.
> Add the BBQ sauce and the lime juice and continue cooking.
> After cornbread has cooled, poke holes and put in the BBQ sauce, chicken and cheddar cheese.
> Bake for another 20 minutes. Serve with scallions.

NUTRITIONAL FACTS:

Serving Size 270 g, Amount Per Serving, Calories 577, Calories from Fat 239, Total Fat 26.5g, Saturated Fat 15.1g, Trans Fat 0.0g, Cholesterol 134mg, Sodium 1494mg, Potassium 373mg, Total Carbohydrates 54.2g, Dietary Fiber 1.7g, Sugars 23.9g, Protein 31.7g

Vitamin A 14%, Vitamin C 8%, Calcium 45%, Iron 11%, Nutrition Grade C-, Based on a 2000 calorie diet

SIZZLING SOUTHWESTERN CHEDDAR CHICKEN–

This is a sizzling chicken recipe that has a little kick. Where is a tortilla when you need one? You can use it to sop up the leftover salsa or cool down your mouth before the next bite. – Wrote this one. Was not included in the original.

Prep Time: 5 Minutes
Cook Time: 25 Minutes
Servings: 4

INGREDIENTS

1 lb. boneless skinless chicken breasts
4oz taco seasoning
1 tsp. cayenne pepper
Kosher salt
2 cloves minced garlic

1 chopped small red onion
2 chopped red bell peppers
15-oz. can black beans (drained)
2 cups shredded cheddar
1/2 cup Chopped fresh cilantro

DIRECTIONS

> Sprinkle the chicken with the taco seasoning, cayenne pepper and salt.
> Add it to the non-stick skillet and cook for 6 minutes on each side. Take chicken out when done.
> Next, add the rest of the ingredients and cook for 7 minutes.
> Re-add chicken to the skillet and cook for 2 minutes with cheese mixture.
> Garnish and serve.

NUTRITIONAL FACTS

Serving Size 386 g, Amount Per Serving, Calories 502, Calories from Fat 148, Total Fat 16.5g, Saturated Fat 6.7g, Trans Fat 0.0g, Cholesterol 122mg, Sodium 1012mg, Potassium 961mg, Total Carbohydrates 30.4g, Dietary Fiber 6.8g, Sugars 4.4g, Protein 56.7g

Vitamin A 50%, Vitamin C 132%, Calcium 35%, Iron 26%
Nutrition Grade B+, Based on a 2000 calorie diet

NUTRITIONAL ANALYSIS / GOOD POINTS

Low in sugar, High in niacin, High in phosphorus, High in selenium, Very high in vitamin C

FIESTA CHICKEN

Fiesta Chicken with Salsa and Peppers is a great way to liven up a normal everyday meal. The peppers and salsa will spice up this dish and will be a great hit with the family. Pair with a margarita or a corona to make for a fun night.

Prep Time: 5 Minutes
Cook Time: 30 Minutes
Servings: 4

INGREDIENTS

1 ¼ cup chicken broth
5oz couscous (box of roasted garlic-and-olive-oil)
2 tsp. vegetable oil
1lb chicken thighs (6 large bone-in, skin-on)
1 ½ tsp. kosher salt
¾ tsp. ground pepper
3 medium bell peppers (colorful)
½ medium onion

2 cloves garlic

(Salsa Verde Ingredients Mix Below)
¼ cup fresh parsley
¼ cup fresh basil
1 green onion
¼ cup extra-virgin olive oil
2 tbsp. capers
1 ½ tbsp. fresh lemon juice

DIRECTIONS

> Boil the chicken broth and add to the couscous. Set aside.
> Place chicken in a non-stick skillet, sprinkle with salt and pepper and cook for 7 minutes on each side.
> Transfer to a plate and add cook peppers for 4 minutes.
> Add the chicken on top of the peppers and bake in the oven on 400 degrees for 10 minutes.
> Put the chicken, onions, capers and lemon juice on top of the couscous and serve.

NUTRITIONAL FACTS:

Serving Size 366 g, Amount Per Serving, Calories 530Calories from Fat 219, Total Fat 24.4g, Saturated Fat 4.8g, Cholesterol 101mg, Sodium 1348mg, Potassium 663mg, Total Carbohydrates 36.0g, Dietary Fiber 4.5g, Sugars 4.8g, Protein 40.4g

Vitamin A 66%, Vitamin C 207%, Calcium 6%, Iron 16%, Nutrition Grade B, Based on a 2000 calorie diet

NUTRITIONAL ANALYSIS / GOOD POINTS

High in niacin, High in vitamin A, Very high in vitamin C

SONOMA MUSHROOM and WINE CHICKEN

Ever dream of cooking in a French kitchen? This easy French chicken will make you feel like you are cooking in one of the top culinary schools in Paris, and with ease. So, take out an electric skillet and spatula, and give it a try.

Prep Time: 5 Minutes
Cook Time: 20 Minutes
Servings: 4

INGREDIENTS

1/2 lb. chicken (3 large cutlets sliced)
Sea salt
Ground pepper
½ cup all-purpose flour
1 medium sliced sweet onion
½ lb. sliced mushrooms

1 sliced yellow bell pepper
1 oz. Tomato paste (about 2 tsps.)
½ cup white wine
½ cup beef broth
14.5 oz. chopped tomatoes (1 can)
½ tsp. butter

DIRECTIONS

> Rub salt, pepper and flour onto the chicken.
> Place the chicken into a non-stick skillet and cook on both sides for 3 minutes.
> Transfer the chicken onto a plate.
> Cook the mushrooms, onions, tomato paste and peppers in the skillet for 7 minutes.
> Add the wine, broth and tomatoes, and cook for 4 minutes.
> Re-Add the chicken and butter when it starts to boil and cook for another 4 minutes
> Serve.

NUTRITIONAL FACTS:

Serving Size 356 g, Amount Per Serving, Calories 233, Calories from Fat 27, Total Fat 3.0g, Saturated Fat 0.9g, Cholesterol 45mg, Sodium 193mg, Potassium 777mg, Total Carbohydrates 24.4g, Dietary Fiber 3.7g, Sugars 7.3g, Protein 22.3g

Vitamin A 38%, Vitamin C 95%, Calcium 3%, Iron 21%, Nutrition Grade B+, Based on a 2000 calorie diet

NUTRITIONAL ANALYSIS / GOOD POINTS

Low in saturated fat, High in niacin, High in selenium, High in vitamin A, Very high in vitamin B6, Very high in vitamin C

SIMPLY ITALIAN MUSHROOM CHICKEN RAVIOLI

Italian chicken ravioli is a fast, easy recipe that is bursting with flavor. The mushrooms, tomatoes, garlic and cheese brings you all the flavor that we have grown accustomed to with Italian food, but without all the hassle in the kitchen.

Prep Time: 15 Minutes
Cook Time: 15 Minutes
Servings: 4

INGREDIENTS

Kosher Salt
9-ounce package of cheese ravioli
1 tbsp. olive oil for drizzling
1 ¼ lbs. boneless, skinless chicken breast cut into chunks
Fresh ground pepper
8 ounces of sliced white mushrooms

1 cup of diced cherry tomatoes
2 cloves of sliced garlic
2 tsp. Red wine vinegar
1/3 cup of chicken broth
2 tsp. Grated parmesan cheese
¼ cup fresh parsley

DIRECTIONS

> Cook ravioli.
> In a non-stick skillet cook the chicken for two minutes on both sides.
> Transfer to a plate.
> Add the mushrooms and tomatoes and cook for 7 minutes.
> Return the chicken, ravioli, chicken broth and parmesan cheese and cook for 5 minutes.
> Garnish and serve.

NUTRITIONAL FACTS:

Serving Size 353 g, Amount Per Serving, Calories 534, Calories from Fat 148, Total Fat 16.5g, Saturated Fat 4.7g, Trans Fat 0.0g, Cholesterol 183mg, Sodium 442mg, Potassium 808mg, Total Carbohydrates 35.9g, Dietary Fiber 1.3g, Sugars 2.3g, Protein 60.6g

Vitamin A 18%, Vitamin C 22%, Calcium 21%, Iron 33%, Nutrition Grade A-, Based on a 2000 calorie diet

NUTRITIONAL ANALYSIS / GOOD POINTS

Low in sugar, Very high in niacin, High in phosphorus, High in selenium, Very high in vitamin B6, High in vitamin B12

CREAMY THICK AND HEARTY SHEPHERD'S PI

The smell of sweet, buttery mashed potatoes blanketing the heaps of chicken and vegetables stirs the hunger within the stomachs. Who said that Shepherd's pie only had to be made with beef? Try this recipe and you will be thankful that you made the switch.

Prep Time: 15 Minutes
Cook Time: 15 Minutes
Servings: 4

INGREDIENTS

2 cups cooked chicken cut into cubes
1 (16-ounce) package frozen mixed vegetables
10.5 oz. cream of mushroom soup (1 can condensed can)

1/2 cup milk
1/4 tsp. onion powder
1/4 tsp. black pepper
4 cups mashed potatoes (hot)

DIRECTIONS -

> In a non-stick skillet put in all ingredients that are listed above, except for the potatoes. Make sure you stir these ingredients after you put them in.
> Cook for 7-8 minutes, remember to stir often. (sauce will thicken while heating)
> Serve over potatoes.

NUTRITIONAL FACTS:

Serving Size 531 g, Amount Per Serving, Calories 428, Calories from Fat 72, Total Fat 8.0g, Saturated Fat 2.7g, Cholesterol 61mg, Sodium 885mg, Potassium 1078mg, Total Carbohydrates 58.1g, Dietary Fiber 5.0g, Sugars 5.5g, Protein 30.8g

Vitamin A 100%, Vitamin C 8%, Calcium 13%, Iron 17%, Nutrition Grade A-, Based on a 2000 calorie diet

NUTRITIONAL ANALYSIS / GOOD POINTS

High in niacin. Very high in vitamin A, High in vitamin B6

TURKEY SMOKED ITALIAN SAUSAGE GARLIC & BASIL PASTA

Italian Sausage made with turkey? This is an abomination. Try this recipe and you will learn to love the flavor and the low-calorie count.

Prep Time: 15 Minutes
Cook Time: 15 Minutes
Servings: 6

INGREDIENTS

1 lb. turkey sausage (1 package sliced)
1/2 cup chopped green bell pepper
14.5 oz. Diced Tomatoes (1 can with Basil, Garlic & Oregano)
1 cup Tomato Sauce

1-1/2 cups water
8 oz. dry uncooked rigatoni pasta
1oz grated Parmesan cheese
1oz parsley (garnish)

DIRECTIONS -

> In a non-stick skillet add the turkey sausage and brown it...cooking for 5 about minutes turning occasionally.
> Add the chopped green peppers to the skillet and cook for 2 more minutes sprinkling a pinch of salt and pepper for flavor.
> Next, combine the water, tomatoes sauce and pasta...bringing it all to a boil.
> Simmer the dish turning the head down and covered for 15 minutes.
> Take the grated parmesan cheese and shower the meal adding the parsley for Garnish.
> Serve while hot.

NUTRITIONAL FACTS:

Serving Size 279 g, Amount Per Serving, Calories 407, Calories from Fat 212, Total Fat 23.6g, Saturated Fat 7.7g, Trans Fat 0.2g, Cholesterol 94mg, Sodium 841mg, Potassium 630mg, Total Carbohydrates 26.5g, Dietary Fiber 1.7g, Sugars 3.9g, Protein 21.9g

Vitamin A 29%, Vitamin C 48%, Calcium 8%, Iron 18%, Nutrition Grade B-, Based on a 2000 calorie diet

NUTRITIONAL ANALYSIS / GOOD POINTS

High in vitamin C

FLAVORED GARLIC PARMESAN TURKEY & BROCCOLI PASTA

Turkey is an overlooked meat if Thanksgiving is not on the mind, especially when a quick dinner is desired. However, it can be a perfect substitute for any of the more thought-about proteins! This entrée pairs the turkey with broccoli and pasta, and with a few spices it will easily convince you that chicken is not the only bird available on weeknights.

Prep Time: 15 Minutes
Cook Time: 20 Minutes
Servings: 4

INGREDIENTS

¾ pound orecchiette
2 cups broccoli florets
3 tablespoons olive oil
1 pound ground turkey
2 cloves garlic, chopped
1/4 cup chopped onion

1 teaspoon fennel seed
½ teaspoon crushed red pepper
kosher salt
1/2 Cup shredded Parmesan + more for serving

DIRECTIONS

> Cook the pasta as directed on the box instructions, and during the final minute of the pasta cooking, add the broccoli. Make sure you drain the water out of the skillet.
> Return all then return to skillet.
> While the pasta a broccoli is cooking, add 1 tablespoon of the oil to your skillet and heat. After the oil is warm, place the rest of the ingredients in the skillet and cook. Make sure you cook for several minutes or until the meat is done, mixing the ingredients while cooking. Add salt as desired.
> Put the turkey and other ingredients into the skillet and mix with the pasta, the other two tablespoons of oil, and broccoli. You may sprinkle the dish with parmesan cheese before serving.

NUTRITIONAL FACTS:

Serving Size 279 g, Amount Per Serving, Calories 706, Calories from Fat 265, Total Fat 29.4g, Saturated Fat 6.6g, Trans Fat 0.0g, Cholesterol 131mg, Sodium 264mg, Potassium 494mg, Total Carbohydrates 70.7g, Dietary Fiber 4.6g, Sugars 4.2g, Protein 45.1g

Vitamin A 10%, Vitamin C 70%, Calcium 16%, Iron 15%, Nutrition Grade B, Based on a 2000 calorie diet

NUTRITIONAL ANALYSIS / GOOD POINTS
Low in sodium, Low in sugar, High in selenium

CREAMY & CHEESY TURKEY ALFREDO WITH SPINACH

Chicken Alfredo is an essential entrée, but a different bird can liven up the party from time to time. Ground Turkey is an excellent change to the dish, but make sure not to ignore the chicken every time! The Italian seasoning keeps the meal true to form, and the spinach and tomatoes add a fresh taste to the creamy classic, making it enjoyable for new and old fans alike.

Prep Time: 10 Minutes
Cook Time: 15 Minutes
Servings: 4

INGREDIENTS

2 cups rotini pasta (6 oz.)
1 lb. lean ground turkey
1 teaspoon Italian seasoning
1/4 teaspoon salt
1/2 crushed red pepper
3 cups firmly packed fresh spinach leaves

1 container (10 oz.) refrigerated reduced-fat Alfredo pasta sauce
1 can (14.5 oz.) petite diced tomatoes, un-drained
1/4 cup shredded Parmesan cheese (1 oz.)

DIRECTIONS

> Using the package directions, cook the pasta to desired liking and drain.
> While the pasta is cooking, cook turkey, Italian seasoning, crushed red pepper, and salt in a nonstick skillet over medium-high heat for approximately 5-7 minutes while stirring. Drain when ready.
> Mix the spinach and turkey together. Leave the electric skillet uncovered and let cook for 2-3 minutes while stirring occasionally, the stir in pasta sauce and tomatoes when you see the spinach is cooked down. Continue to stir for just a few minutes and then finally add the pasta.
> Add cheese, cover, melting the cheese cooking for about 3-5 minutes on a low temperature.

NUTRITIONAL FACTS:

Serving Size 361 g, Amount Per Serving, Calories 634, Calories from Fat 225, Total Fat 25.0g, Saturated Fat 12.1g, Trans Fat 0.0g, Cholesterol 146mg, Sodium 3761mg, Potassium 836mg, Total Carbohydrates 62.2g, Dietary Fiber 1.9g, Sugars 3.0g, Protein 40.9g

Vitamin A 65%, Vitamin C 35%, Calcium 11%, Iron 24%, Nutrition Grade C, Based on a 2000 calorie diet

NUTRITIONAL ANALYSIS / GOOD POINTS
Low in sugar

THE FRESHEST, EASIEST GARLIC CHICKEN IN THE COOP

Quick and simple: two great words to hear regarding entrees. This chicken dish uses the most basic of ingredients, and provides mouth-watering taste. Luckily for any cook, the elements to this entrée may already be in the kitchen, which makes this meal perfect if time is an issue and a hungry family waits.

Prep Time: 12 Minutes
Cook Time: 15-25 Minutes
Servings: 4 Servings

INGREDIENTS

1 1/2 lbs. chicken breasts (Boneless and skinless)
4 Garlic cloves, minced
1/4 cup chopped onions
1/4 teaspoon lemon juice

4 Tablespoons of brown sugar
1 Tablespoon of olive oil
1 Tablespoon of salt
1 Tablespoon of ground pepper
*Add spices as desired

DIRECTIONS

> Turn the oven on to 450°F to get nice and warm.
> Sauté garlic and onions with lemon juice and olive oil in a small nonstick electric skillet.
> Take the electric skillet off the heat and add the brown sugar.
> Use salt and pepper to season the chicken to your liking.
> Coat the chicken with the garlic and brown sugar mixture and then place the breasts in the oven.
> Bake the dish for 20-25 minutes. Make sure to keep checking the chicken because the cooking time may vary on the size of your chicken breasts. Use a knife to cut into the chicken to check it.

NUTRITIONAL FACTS:

Serving Size 199 g, Amount Per Serving, Calories 399, Calories from Fat 146, Total Fat 16.2g, Saturated Fat 4.0g, Cholesterol 151mg, Sodium 1894mg, Potassium 469mg, Total Carbohydrates 11.5g, Dietary Fiber 0.6g, Sugars 9.1g, Protein 49.7g
Vitamin A 2%, Vitamin C 3%, Calcium 5%, Iron 15%, Nutrition Grade B-, Based on a 2000 calorie diet

NUTRITIONAL ANALYSIS / GOOD POINTS

High in niacin, High in selenium, High in vitamin B6

MEATLOVER'S ROASTED CHICKEN WITH SAUTEED PROSCIUTTO

This entrée is a light and fresh mixture of meat and vegetables. Using basic ingredients, the dish provides tastes everyone can recognize and enjoy. The chicken and Zucchini complement each other well and the prosciutto adds a salty, flavorful presence to the main course. The citrus from the lemon gives a perfect end to a dish that electric skillets many flavors, but in little time!

Prep Time: 15 Minutes
Cook Time: 15 Minutes
Servings: 4

INGREDIENTS

2 lbs. chicken breasts (About 4 Boneless and skinless)
1/2 teaspoon kosher salt
1/2 teaspoon black pepper
2 tablespoons olive oil
1/4-pound (about 8 slices) prosciutto

2 small zucchini, thinly sliced into half-moons
1 small yellow squash
1 red pepper, sliced
1 clove garlic, thinly sliced
2 oz. lemon (zest and juice)

DIRECTIONS

〉 Use the lemon zest and a pinch each of salt and pepper to season the chicken.
〉 In your skillet, heat 1 tablespoon of the oil over medium-high heat, Heat the chicken up till it starts to look done. Probably cooking for about a couple of minutes on each side.
〉 Afterwards, turn the temperature to 400 degrees and bake it for approximately 7-10 minutes.
〉 During this time, add the remaining oil in another electric skillet. Cook the prosciutto on medium for just a couple of minutes on each side, then place on a clean plate. You know it's done when it starts to get crispy.
〉 Mix in and cook the zucchini, squash, red pepper, garlic cooking for 3 minutes in the skillet. Make sure you add salt and pepper to add flavor.
〉 When done, add everything to the chicken. Take the lemon and shower the lemon juice all over the dish and serve.

NUTRITIONAL FACTS:

Serving Size 397 g, Amount Per Serving, Calories 561, Calories from Fat 231, Total Fat 25.7g

Saturated Fat 6.2g, Cholesterol 217mg, Sodium 837mg, Potassium 953mg, Total Carbohydrates 6.9g, Dietary Fiber 2.1g, Sugars 3.1g, Protein 73.1g

Vitamin A 25%, Vitamin C 101%, Calcium 6%, Iron 21%, Nutrition Grade B+, Based on a 2000 calorie diet

NUTRITIONAL ANALYSIS / GOOD POINTS

Low in sugar, High in niacin, High in selenium, High in vitamin B6, High in vitamin C

Chapter 11:
FISH:

Try any one of these light, flakey and delicious calorie counting entrees that will make float your boat. This is a great way to learn techniques that will perk up your plate and give you the healthy meal that your tummy is craving and deserves! So...turn a few of the pages, even with your eyes closed, and just pick-a-dish! You will be satisfied with any choice in this section! And after you've tried a few...you'll know that we've casted the lines and "Reeled You In!"

ELECTRIC SKILLET-FRIED BAYOU GARLIC CATFISH

Catfish is a Southern staple and a delightful entrée for many occasions. Despite the norm, there is no need for a deep fryer when it comes to this blackened course; the spices will exercise your senses fine on their own and in a healthier fashion. Quick, easy, delicious, and without the mess of batter; what else could you ask for?

Prep Time: 15 Minutes
Cook Time: 10 Minutes
Servings: 6

INGREDIENTS

1.5 tablespoons paprika
1/2 tablespoon cayenne pepper
2.5 teaspoons salt
2 teaspoons lemon pepper
1.5 teaspoons garlic powder
1 teaspoons ground pepper

1/2 teaspoon red pepper
1.5 teaspoons dried basil
1 teaspoon onion powder
1 teaspoon thyme
6 catfish fillets
1 cup unsalted butter, melted

DIRECTIONS

› Place an electric skillet or skillet over medium high heat.
› Stir all the spices together in a mixing container.
› Melt butter. Dip the catfish to use it as a base to coat both sides of fish with a little bit of the spice mixture for each fillet. After seasoning, let the rest on wax paper.
› After placing the fish in a hot electric skillet, divide and drizzle the remaining melted butter over each filet.
› Cook the fish until desired liking or when starting to brown or flaky Just a few minutes on each side. Serve hot. Mmmmmmm...delicious.
›

NUTRITIONAL FACTS:

Serving Size 205 g, Amount Per Serving, Calories 501, Calories from Fat 389, Total Fat 43.2g, Saturated Fat 21.7g, Cholesterol 157mg, Sodium 1273mg, Potassium 600mg, Total Carbohydrates 2.9g, Dietary Fiber 1.2g, Sugars 0.6g, Protein 25.8g

Vitamin A 43%, Vitamin C 6%, Calcium 4%, Iron 13%, Nutrition Grade D+, Based on a 2000 calorie diet

NUTRITIONAL ANALYSIS / GOOD POINTS

Very low in sugar, High in vitamin B12

SAVORY BASIL SHRIMP AND CHEESY GNOCCHI

Shrimp is a Superfood, and Italians know their way around a kitchen; it's time for you to experience the best of both, and all you will need is a skillet! The most difficult part of this meal is finding good gnocchi, but it shouldn't be too hard to come across. After your shopping is done, mix the shrimp, gnocchi, vegetables, and classic herbs and spices and you have a full course meal ready to serve in one dish.

Prep Time: 15 Minutes
Cook Time: 15 Minutes
Servings: 4

INGREDIENTS

1 tablespoon plus 2 teaspoons extra-virgin olive oil, divided
1 16-ounce package shelf-stable gnocchi
1/2 cup sliced shallots
1 bunch asparagus (about 1 pound), trimmed and cut into thirds
3/4 cup reduced-sodium chicken broth

1 pound raw shrimp (26-30 per pound), peeled and deveined, tails left on if desired
1/4 teaspoon freshly ground pepper
Pinch of salt
1 teaspoon oregano
1 teaspoon basil
2 tablespoons lemon juice
1/3 cup grated Parmesan cheese
1/3 cup grated Romano cheese
1/3 cup grated mozzarella cheese

DIRECTIONS

> Put 1 tablespoon oil and add gnocchi to skillet and heat the electric skillet. Cook anywhere between 5 and 10 minutes. Make sure you stirring continuously. Then place in clean container.
> Put the oil and add shallots to the same electric skillet. Keep the heat on medium and cook for a few minutes, stirring occasionally. Add the asparagus and put in broth and let cook covered for several more minutes. Add shrimp, spices, salt and pepper. Re-cover and bring to a simmer for another few minutes. Check that the shrimp is cooked!
> Put in the lemon juice, and the gnocchi back to the skillet and put. Cook and stir for just a couple of minutes then take away from heat and use all cheeses to smother the top. Cover and simmer until cheese has melted.
> Yummy for your tummy! ;)

NUTRITIONAL FACTS:
Serving Size 448 g, Amount Per Serving, Calories 400, Calories from Fat 120, Total Fat 13.4g, Saturated Fat 4.6g, Trans Fat 0.0g, Cholesterol 254mg, Sodium 642mg, Potassium 1022mg, Total Carbohydrates 30.9g, Dietary Fiber 5.1g, Sugars 3.3g, Protein 40.1g

Vitamin A 34%, Vitamin C 57%, Calcium 36%, Iron 23%, Nutrition Grade A, Based on a 2000 calorie diet

NUTRITIONAL ANALYSIS / GOOD POINTS
Low in sugar, High in phosphorus, High in vitamin B12, High in vitamin C

SEARED JALAPEÑO SALMON SNAP PEA SLAW

Say that five times fast! It's a mouthful, and so is this dish. The flavors are wonderful together: jalapeno, cilantro, ginger, lime, and rice vinegar. Salmon of course is one of the savory fish to cook as well! This course takes little time to prepare which is good because your mouth will be watering until it is served.

Prep Time: 10 Minutes
Cook Time: 5 Minutes
Servings: 4

INGREDIENTS

8 oz. snap peas, trimmed and sliced
.5 oz. jalapeño (about 1/2 - red and chopped)
3 tbsp. Fresh cilantro, chopped
1 tbsp. fresh ginger, grated
1 tbsp. fresh lemon juice

1 tbsp. rice vinegar
1 tbsp. olive oil
2 tsp. soy sauce
Kosher salt
Freshly ground black pepper
4 Salmon fillets.

DIRECTIONS

> Add oil to an electric skillet over medium high heat.
> Add the snap peas to the electric skillet then mix in the red jalapeño, fresh cilantro, fresh ginger, and lastly put in the fresh lemon juice, rice vinegar, canola oil, and soy sauce.
> While the slaw is cooking, sear the salmon.
> Use the salt and pepper to season the slaw.
> Serve together.
>

NUTRITION FACTS

Serving Size 254 g, Amount Per Serving, Calories 322, Calories from Fat 134, Total Fat 14.8g, Saturated Fat 2.2g, Trans Fat 0.0g, Cholesterol 78mg, Sodium 271mg, Potassium 862mg, Total Carbohydrates 9.7g, Dietary Fiber 3.2g, Sugars 3.5g. Protein 38.0g

Vitamin A 13%, Vitamin C 44%, Calcium 8%, Iron 12%, Nutrition Grade B+, Based on a 2000 calorie diet

NUTRITIONAL ANALYSIS / GOOD POINTS

Very high in magnesium, Very high in phosphorus, Very high in selenium, High in vitamin C

TANTALIZING TILAPIA IN GARLIC
AND FRESH TOMATOES

One of the most basic and adaptable fish, Tilapia can be easily acquired and cooked into a savory meal. With this entrée, the fish is soaked and seared in tomato, wine, olive, and garlic. Many of the ingredients are common and can be found in most kitchens, but make sure to buy enough wine for the fish and you to share! Quick and easy!

Prep Time: 10 Minutes
Cook Time: 10 Minutes
Servings: 4

INGREDIENTS

1 1/4 pounds tilapia
1/4 teaspoon salt
1/4 teaspoon freshly ground pepper
3 tablespoons cilantro
2.5 oz. lime (fresh zest and juice.)

2 tablespoons extra-virgin olive oil, divided
1 pint grape or cherry tomatoes, halved if large
1/4 cup dry white wine
3 cloves garlic, finely chopped

DIRECTIONS

> Season the fish with salt, pepper, cilantro, and zest of lime.
> Add 1 tablespoon oil in a skillet over medium-high heat. Cook the fish half way the turn on other side, about 5 minutes or so, then transfer the tilapia to a clean plate and place under foil. You can add a pinch of salt and pepper just for hint of flavor.
> Add the rest of the ingredients after turning off the heat to the electric skillet. Cover on medium heat; cook the mixture for no more than 5 minutes, stirring occasionally. Put the sauce over the fish. Add parsley garnish if desired.

NUTRITIONAL FACTS:

Serving Size 231 g, Amount Per Serving, Calories 229, Calories from Fat 76, Total Fat 8.5g, Saturated Fat 1.6g, Trans Fat 0.0g, Cholesterol 69mg, Sodium 200mg, Potassium 135mg, Total Carbohydrates 11.0g, Dietary Fiber 1.0g, Sugars 7.9g, Protein 27.0g

Vitamin A 2%, Vitamin C 13%, Calcium 4%, Iron 10%, Nutrition Grade D, Based on a 2000 calorie diet

ELECTRIC SKILLET-FRIED GARLIC PARMESEAN TUNA CAKES

That's right, not crab cakes, but tuna cakes! Though the Maryland delicacy is a great entrée, there can be variations within the seafood family. These tuna patties are perfect for dinner and for lunch, and are easy enough to make at any time for you or a group. Dip in some hot sauce for extra spicy flavor!

Prep Time: 15 Minutes
Cook Time: 10 Minutes
Servings: 8

INGREDIENTS

2 eggs
2 teaspoons lemon juice
¾ cup bread crumbs (Italian seasoned)
3 (6 oz.) cans tuna, drained
¼ cup diced onion

2 cloves of garlic, minced
1 teaspoon oregano
1 teaspoon basil
1 pinch ground black pepper
3 tablespoons olive oil

DIRECTIONS

⟩ To make the paste, whisk the eggs in a small container along with the lemon juice together before stirring in the bread crumbs and parmesan cheese. Add onions and garlic, stir, and then fold in Tuna until mixed is combined. Season the fish with black pepper, oregano, and basil, and then separate into about 8 full sized patties.

⟩ Add oil to skillet and fry each patty…each side will be about 4-5 minutes; you will know when they are done when you see them turn a light crisp brown in color.

NUTRITIONAL FACTS:

Serving Size 96 g, Amount Per Serving, Calories 223, Calories from Fat 109, Total Fat 12.1g, Saturated Fat 2.3g, Cholesterol 61mg, Sodium 122mg, Potassium 260mg, Total Carbohydrates 8.1g, Dietary Fiber 0.7g, Sugars 0.9g, Protein 19.8g

Vitamin A 2%, Vitamin C 2%, Calcium 3%, Iron 7%, Nutrition Grade B-, Based on a 2000 calorie diet

NUTRITIONAL ANALYSIS / GOOD POINTS

Low in sugar, High in niacin, Very high in selenium, High in vitamin B12

RED HOT GARLIC PARMESAN SHRIMP SKILLET PASTA

There are not too many ways to go wrong with shrimp and this recipe isn't one of them. Pairing spinach, basil, sweet peas and pesto make a great and easy Italian dish

Prep Time: 5 Minutes
Cook Time: 35 Minutes
Servings: 8

INGREDIENTS

12oz Rotini Pasta (can substitute with penne pasta)
1oz parmesan cheese (grated)
¼ cup pine nuts
1 chopped clove garlic
1 tsp. Sea salt

1 tsp. Freshly ground black pepper
1 lb. shrimp (peeled and deveined medium)
1 cup peas
Pinch of crushed red pepper
1 tsp. chili flakes for garnish

DIRECTIONS

›	Prepare pesto in a food blender for an easy mix: add spinach, basil, parmesan cheese, pine nuts, garlic crushed red pepper, salt and pepper.
›	Add shrimp to a non-stick skillet and cook for 4 minutes or till you see the shrimp is cooked.
›	Add cooked pasta, peas and pesto. Combine ¼ cup water to skillet stirring occasionally until the sauce richens up.
›	Garnish with cheese, chili flakes and serve.

NUTRITIONAL FACTS

Serving Size 126 g, Amount Per Serving, Calories 246, Calories from Fat 51, Total Fat 5.7g, Saturated Fat 1.2g, Trans Fat 0.0g, Cholesterol 153mg, Sodium 418mg, Potassium 248mg, Total Carbohydrates 27.8g, Dietary Fiber 1.2g, Sugars 1.2g, Protein 20.5g

Vitamin A 7%, Vitamin C 13%, Calcium 10%, Iron 12%, Nutrition Grade B+, Based on a 2000 calorie diet

NUTRITIONAL ANALYSIS / GOOD POINTS

Low in sugar, High in phosphorus

ITALIAN BASIL FRIED FISH

Ever fried fish in a skillet without oil or butter? With the non-stick electric skillet, you don't need butter or oil. This is an easy way to re-create a dish with delicious taste

Prep Time: 5 Minutes
Cook Time: 25 Minutes
Servings: 4

INGREDIENTS

1 tbsp. traditional basil pesto sauce
1 chopped yellow pepper
1 chopped zucchini

1 cup grape tomatoes
3 tbsp. diced fresh basil

DIRECTIONS

- Dress the fish with dressing.
- Add fish to a non-stick skillet and cook for 3 minutes on each side. (You will see the fish start to flake when done)
- Move to plate and make sure to keep the fish warm.
- Add pesto, vegetables and the rest of the dressing, to the skillet. Keep stirring and cook for about five minutes.
- Garnish with basil and serve over cooked pasta.

NUTRITIONAL FACTS:

Serving Size 146 g, Amount Per Serving, Calories 46, Calories from Fat 17, Total Fat 1.9g, Trans Fat 0.0g, Cholesterol 1mg, Sodium 32mg, Potassium 339mg, Total Carbohydrates 6.6g, Dietary Fiber 1.6g, Sugars 2.3g, Protein 1.9g

Vitamin A 14%, Vitamin C 167%, Calcium 3%, Iron 3%, Nutrition Grade A, Based on a 2000 calorie diet

NUTRITIONAL ANALYSIS / GOOD POINTS

Very low in cholesterol, High in dietary fiber, High in manganese, High in magnesium, Very high in potassium, Very high in vitamin A, Very high in vitamin B6, Very high in vitamin C

KICKIN ARTIC CHAR

Char is a great substitute for Salmon or trout, especially for those who want to protect the environment. For those who like mild types of fish, this is the recipe for you, and you can finish it off with a kick.

Prep Time: 5 Minutes
Cook Time: 30 Minutes
Servings: 4

INGREDIENTS

1/4 cup shallots (large diced)
1 cup chicken broth
1/4 cup water
1 lb. chopped kale
1 lb. arctic char (skinned & cut into 4 portions)

1/4 tsp. salt
1/4 tsp. freshly ground pepper
1/4 cup reduced-fat the cream
2 tsp. prepared horseradish
1 tbsp. chopped fresh dill
4 lemon wedges for garnish

DIRECTIONS

> Create Sauce: combine dill, horseradish and the cream in a mixing bowl.
> Add shallots to a non-stick electric skillet and cook for 2 minutes.
> Next, add the broth, water and half the kale and cook for 10 minutes.
> Season the fish with salt and pepper and add to the skillet. Cook for 7 minutes.
> Serve the fish over cooked pasta, with the sauce and garnish with lemon wedges.
>

NUTRITIONAL FACTS:

Serving Size 330 g, Amount Per Serving, Calories 283, Calories from Fat 79, Total Fat 8.8g, Saturated Fat 3.3g, Trans Fat 0.0g, Cholesterol 101mg, Sodium 494mg, Potassium 697mg, Total Carbohydrates 15.2g, Dietary Fiber 1.9g, Protein 8.2g

Vitamin A 357%, Vitamin C 231%, Calcium 19%, Iron 17%, Nutrition Grade B, Based on a 2000 calorie diet

NUTRITIONAL ANALYSIS / GOOD POINTS

Very low in sugar, High in manganese, Very high in vitamin A, Very high in vitamin C

SANTA CRUZ STYLE CLAMBAKE

This is a perfect recipe for those who are craving a beachside classic. The clambake is not reserved to when you go to the seashore, but can be made right here, "right now" in your very own kitchen anytime.

Prep Time: 20 Minutes
Cook Time: 20 Minutes
Servings: 4

INGREDIENTS

3 cups water
1 tablespoon seafood seasoning
1 dozen red potatoes (12 potatoes)
3 ears fresh corn
1 tsp. salt

2 dozen cleaned littleneck clams (2 lbs.)
1/4 cup melted butter
parsley for garnish

DIRECTIONS

› In a non-stick skillet add water, seasoning, potatoes, corn and salt and cook for 20 min.
› Add clams, cover and cook for 5 minutes. (When clams are ready they will open!)
› Warning: throw away any clams that do not open.
› Garnish with parsley and serve with melted butter.

NUTRITIONAL FACTS:

Serving Size 1116 g, Amount Per Serving, Calories 706, Calories from Fat 119, Total Fat 13.3g, Saturated Fat 7.6g, Cholesterol 31mg, Sodium 1529mg, Potassium 3263mg, Total Carbohydrates 138.1g, Dietary Fiber 13.5g, Sugars 15.6g, Protein 15.2g

Vitamin A 15%, Vitamin C 116%, Calcium 10%, Iron 38%, Nutrition Grade B+, Based on a 2000 calorie diet

NUTRITIONAL ANALYSIS / GOOD POINTS

Low in cholesterol, High in potassium, Very high in vitamin B6, High in vitamin C

HERB CRUSTED COD WITH VEGETABLES

This is a fast and easy dinner that you can make on a regular basis. The kids will love the flavor and you will enjoy the small clean-up. It's a win-win for everyone.

Prep Time: 15 Minutes
Cook Time: 15 Minutes
Servings: 4

INGREDIENTS

1/4 cup water
2 tsps. dry white wine
1/2 teaspoon thyme
ground black pepper
1 large diced carrot

2 stalks diced celery
1 diced small onion
1 can Condensed Cream of Mushroom Soup
4 firm cod fillets

DIRECTIONS

> In a non-stick electric skillet bring the water and wine to a boil.
> Then add thyme, black pepper, carrot, celery and onion
> Cover and simmer for 5 minutes.
> Add the soup, and the fish to the skillet. Put the lid on the skillet and cook for 5 more minutes.
> Garnish and serve.

NUTRITIONAL FACTS:

There are no nutritional facts for this recipe

SPICED HALIBUT WITH CORN SUCCOTASH

Halibut with Corn Succotash is a refreshing summer dish to cook on a hot day when you want to mix what it is in season. This dish will not disappoint. Light...Healthy and Delicious!

Prep Time: 15 Minutes
Cook Time: 15 Minutes
Servings: 4

INGREDIENTS

12 oz. can whole kernel corn,
2 peppers (red and green - mix with corn)
2 tsps. sliced green onions (2 medium)
2 tsps. chopped fresh cilantro
½ tsp. ground cumin

1 tsp. Lime juice
1 tsp. honey
¼ tsp. ground cumin
1/8 tsp. pepper
1/8 tsp. sea salt
4 halibut fillets

DIRECTIONS

> Prepare Succotash: put all succotash ingredients into a mixing bowl.
> Cover the fish in cumin adding salt and pepper on both sides.
> In a non-stick skillet cook the fish for 4 minutes on each side till it starts browning and flakes easily.
> Garnish and serve with succotash mixture...Yummy!

NUTRITIONAL FACTS:

Serving Size 157 g, Amount Per Serving, Calories 406, Calories from Fat 67, Total Fat 7.4g, Saturated Fat 1.0g, Cholesterol 93mg, Sodium 218mg, Potassium 1623mg, Total Carbohydrates 21.1g, Dietary Fiber 3.1g, Sugars 5.6g, Protein 63.3g

Vitamin A 5%, Vitamin C 89%, Calcium 3%, Iron 87%, Nutrition Grade A, Based on a 2000 calorie diet

NUTRITIONAL ANALYSIS / GOOD POINTS

Low in saturated fat, Low in sodium, Very high in iron, High in magnesium, Very high in niacin, High in phosphorus, High in potassium, Very high in selenium, Very high in vitamin B6, Very high in vitamin B12, Very high in vitamin C

MEDITERRANEAN GARLIC JALAPENO WHITEFISH

This Mediterranean Garlic Jalapeno Whitefish is a nice-n-light, cool and refreshing dish. One that you can complete in no time.

Prep Time: 30 Minutes
Cook Time: 30 Minutes
Servings: 2

INGREDIENTS

1 large diced tomato
1 diced small green pepper
1 diced jalapeno pepper
3 tsp. Chopped fresh basil
3 tsp. White wine or chicken broth

1 diced shallot
1 diced garlic clove
1 tbsp. Chili powder
2 whitefish fillets

DIRECTIONS

> Prepare tomato mixture: Combine tomatoes, peppers, basil, wine, shallot, garlic and chili powder in s mixing container.
> Season the fish with chili powder.
> In a non-stick skillet cook the fish (until brown and flakey) for 4 minutes on each side.
> Add the tomato mixture at the last 2 minutes of cooking.
> Garnish and serve.
>

NUTRITIONAL FACTS:

Serving Size 302 g, Amount Per Serving, Calories 257, Calories from Fat 76, Total Fat 8.4g, Saturated Fat 1.5g, Cholesterol 31mg, Sodium 507mg, Potassium 1394mg, Total, Carbohydrates 36.2g, Dietary Fiber 18.5g, Sugars 9.2g, Protein 20.4g

Vitamin A 288%, Vitamin C 132%, Calcium 16%, Iron 41%, Nutrition Grade A-, Based on a 2000 calorie diet

NUTRITIONAL ANALYSIS / GOOD POINTS

Very high in dietary fiber, High in iron, High in manganese, High in magnesium, High in niacin, High in phosphorus, High in potassium, High in selenium, Very high in vitamin A, Very high in vitamin B6, Very high in vitamin C

CHAPTER 12:
PORK:

Pork...the other white meat! You know, a lot of people shy away from this delicious flavorful meat, but the reality is...this category of meat is probably the most flavorful of all! Whether cooking an entrée or just adding a little to a meal to give the most perfect flavor, or adding a savory twits to a dish...you will adore the recipes we have custom created for you and yours!

BAKED HOT ITALIAN SAUSAGE, FTHE CHEESY ROTONI

You're in the mood for some of Grandma's home cooking, but you don't want to slave in the kitchen all day long. Then this dish is perfect for you and your family. It's taking a memory from your childhood and putting your own spin on it, without compromising on the taste. That's the most important part after all.

Prep Time: 10 Minutes
Cook Time: 10 Minutes
Servings: 8

INGREDIENTS

1-pound rotini (penne pasta if desired)
3/4 pound hot Italian sausage
2 sweet red peppers
1 onion (see Note)
26 ounces marinara sauce (1 jar)

2 cups shredded Italian four-cheese blend
Tablespoon of Basil
Pinch of crushed red peppers (to add a little kick!)

DIRECTIONS -

> Cook Pasta.
> Slice the sausage, peppers and onions and add to a non-stick skillet.
> Cook for 10 minutes adding the pinch of crushed red peppers.
> Add sauce and basil to the dish and simmer.
> Next, add in the drained pasta and the cheese.
> Bake at 400 degrees for 7 minutes.
> Cool and serve.

NUTRITIONAL FACTS:

Serving Size 263 g, Amount Per Serving, Calories 553, Calories from Fat 222, Total Fat 24.7g, Saturated Fat 10.6g, Trans Fat 0.1g, Cholesterol 67mg, Sodium 873mg, Potassium 528mg, Total Carbohydrates 58.2g, Dietary Fiber 5.3g, Sugars 11.5g, Protein 24.7g

Vitamin A 34%, Vitamin C 69%, Calcium 25%, Iron 22%, Nutrition Grade B-, Based on a 2000 calorie diet

NUTRITIONAL ANALYSIS / GOOD POINTS

High in vitamin C

SPICY SKILET PORK & BACON FRIED RICE

In the mood for Asian tonight, but don't want to order take out. Here is a way for you to learn how to make one of your favorite dishes, so that you can continue to make it over and over again.

Prep Time: 15 Minutes
Cook Time: 15 Minutes
Servings: 4

INGREDIENTS

3/4 lb. boneless pork loin
6oz bacon (6 slices)
1 onion diced or cut into strips
1 cup diced mushrooms
2 eggs

3 cups cold cooked rice
2 tablespoons soy sauce
3 tablespoons chicken broth
1 tablespoon of crushed red peppers

DIRECTIONS

› In a non-stick skillet cook the pork and stir-fry until brown. Remove the pork.
› Cook onions and mushrooms for 5 minutes.
› Add beaten eggs to the skillet and cook until they start setting.
› Lastly, add the cooked pork, cooked bacon, rice, soy sauce, and broth to skillet and cook for 6 minutes or until you see the eggs start to texture.
› Garnish and add fresh ground pepper for added flavor…serve.

NUTRITIONAL FACTS:

Serving Size 354 g, Amount Per Serving, Calories 915, Calories from Fat 218, Total Fat 24.2g, Saturated Fat 7.8g, Trans Fat 0.0g, Cholesterol 191mg, Sodium 1558mg, Potassium 937mg, Total Carbohydrates 116.3g, Dietary Fiber 3.0g, Sugars 2.1g, Protein 52.4g

Vitamin A 14%, Vitamin C 6%, Calcium 7%, Iron 49%, Nutrition Grade B, Based on a 2000 calorie diet

NUTRITIONAL ANALYSIS / GOOD POINTS

Very low in sugar, High in selenium, High in thiamin, High in vitamin B6

SWEET and SAVORY GARLIC PORK

This is a perfect meal to make your kids fall in love with their vegetables. The mouthwatering pork, paired with soy sauce will give that salted pork taste that everyone loves.

Prep Time: 20 Minutes
Cook Time: 20 Minutes
Servings: 4

INGREDIENTS

1 lb. pork tenderloin, cut into strips
16 oz. stir fry vegetables (yellow, red and green peppers, onions)
1/4 cup Sesame Oil (Asian Toasted Dressing)

2 tbsp. soy sauce
1/2 tsp. garlic powder
2 cups broccoli slaw

DIRECTIONS

> In a non-stick skillet add the stripped pork tenderloin and cook for 5 minutes till it is cooked through.
> Add stir-fry and cook for 5 more minutes.
> Put in soy sauce, dressing, garlic powder and cook for 2 minutes.
> Turn off heat and put in broccoli and serve.

NUTRITIONAL FACTS:

Serving Size 294 g, Amount Per Serving, Calories 342, Calories from Fat 160, Total Fat 17.8g, Saturated Fat 3.3g, Trans Fat 0.0g, Cholesterol 83mg, Sodium 546mg, Potassium 872mg, Total Carbohydrates 11.5g, Dietary Fiber 4.3g, Sugars 4.1g, Protein 33.0g

Vitamin A 75%, Vitamin C 106%, Calcium 3%, Iron 16%, Nutrition Grade A-, Based on a 2000 calorie diet

NUTRITIONAL ANALYSIS / GOOD POINTS

High in niacin, Very high in selenium, Very high in thiamin, Very high in vitamin A, High in vitamin B6, Very high in vitamin C

HAWAIIN PINAPPLE SAUTEED PORK

Experience the taste of the islands from your very own kitchen. Teaming pineapples, and thyme together will make you feel like you are strolling on the beach and have your taste-buds screaming for more.

Prep Time: 30 Minutes
Cook Time: 30 Minutes
Servings: 4

INGREDIENTS

1oz pineapple jam (3 tablespoons preserves)
3 tablespoons orange juice
2 teaspoons Dijon mustard
1/2 teaspoon minced fresh ginger
1/2 teaspoon curry powder
8 oz. pineapples (4 fresh or canned pineapple rings - 1/2 inch-thick and cut in half, save any remaining juice)
4 5-ounce boneless pork loin chops (1/2 inch thick), trimmed
2 tablespoons chopped fresh thyme (see Tip), divided
1/2 teaspoon salt, divided
1/4 teaspoon freshly ground pepper, divided

DIRECTIONS

> Create sauce: Preserves, orange juice, mustard, ginger and curry powder in a mixing bowl. Set aside.
> Add the pork chops into non-stick skillet and cover with thyme, salt and pepper.
> Cook for 3 minutes on each side.
> Put the preserve juice and cook for 3 minutes longer.
> Transfer to a plate.
> Add the pineapple and the sauce to the electric skillet. Cook for 2 minutes.
> Serve on top of the pork.

NUTRITIONAL FACTS:

Serving Size 222 g, Amount Per Serving, Calories 263, Calories from Fat 48, Total Fat 5.3g, Saturated Fat 1.8g, Trans Fat 0.1g, Cholesterol 103mg, Sodium 404mg, Potassium 710mg, Total Carbohydrates 14.9g, Dietary Fiber 1.6g, Sugars 10.1g, Protein 37.8g

Vitamin A 2%, Vitamin C 64%, Calcium 5%, Iron 21%, Nutrition Grade A, Based on a 2000 calorie diet

NUTRITIONAL ANALYSIS / GOOD POINTS

High in manganese, Very high in niacin, High in phosphorus, High in riboflavin, Very high in selenium, Very high in thiamin, Very high in vitamin B6, Very high in vitamin C

HONEY CRUNCH PECAN PORK

It's one of those school nights and you have to whip up something fast and delicious that the whole family will love? Well, then this is the recipe for you. This skillet fried pork cutlets are super-fast to make and will leave you licking your plate and asking for more.

Prep Time: 15 Minutes
Cook Time: 15 Minutes
Servings: 4

INGREDIENTS

1/3 cup all-purpose flour
1 teaspoon salt
1/2 teaspoon black pepper
20oz boneless pork loin chops
(4 average pork chops)
4 tablespoons butter, divided

1/4 cup finely chopped onion
1oz pecans (chopped)
1/4 cup honey
1/4 cup chicken broth
1 teaspoon lemon juice

DIRECTIONS

> Cover the pork in the flour, salt and pepper. (meat prep)
> Add the pork to a non-stick skillet and cook for 4-5 minutes on each side until it starts to get a little crispy.
> Transfer to a plate and keep warm.
> Add the butter, onions, and pecans for 6 minutes.
> Add the rest of the ingredients and cook for several minutes more simmering.
> Serve with sauce over the top of the pork chops.

Excellent dish to dip sourdough bread with!

NUTRITIONAL FACTS:

Serving Size 220 g, Amount Per Serving, Calories 462, Calories from Fat 196, Total Fat 21.8g, Saturated Fat 9.5g, Trans Fat 0.1g, Cholesterol 134mg, Sodium 793mg, Potassium 680mg, Total Carbohydrates 27.4g, Dietary Fiber 1.3g, Sugars 18.1g, Protein 39.5g

Vitamin A 7%, Vitamin C 2%, Calcium 2%, Iron 14%, Nutrition Grade B-, Based on a 2000 calorie diet

NUTRITIONAL ANALYSIS / GOOD POINTS

High in niacin, Very high in selenium, Very high in thiamin, High in vitamin B6

THE AMAZING TABASCO PORK
AND BEANS SKILLET

The Amazing Tabasco Pork and Beans Skillet is a one skillet meal. This is a dish where you can add all your ingredients to one skillet and it not only builds flavor, but it makes for an easy clean up!

Prep Time: 10 Minutes
Cook Time: 10 Minutes
Ser**vings:** 2

INGREDIENTS

1/2-pound boneless pork chops, 3/4-inch-thick (about 2 chops)
1/3 cup chopped onion
1/3 cup chopped celery

16 oz.) of Pork and Beans (1 can)
2 teaspoons packed brown sugar
1 tablespoon Tabasco sauce
Parsley for garnish

DIRECTIONS

⟩ In a non-stick skillet cook the pork chops for 10 minutes or till they start to crisp.
⟩ Transfer pork chops to a plate then and cook the celery and onion for 2 minutes.
⟩ Stir in the pork and beans, and brown sugar and Tabasco sauce. Bring to a boil.
⟩ Return the pork chops, cover and simmer for 5 minutes.
⟩ Garnish with parsley and serve.

NUTRITIONAL FACTS:

Serving Size 386 g, Amount Per Serving, Calories 255Calories from Fat 39, Total Fat 4.4g, Saturated Fat 1.4g, Trans Fat 0.0g, Cholesterol 83mg, Sodium 139mg, Potassium 1037mg, Total Carbohydrates 21.5g, Dietary Fiber 8.4g, Sugars 7.1g, Protein 34.2g

Vitamin A 35%, Vitamin C 65%, Calcium 11%, Iron 21%, Nutrition Grade A, Based on a 2000 calorie diet

NUTRITIONAL ANALYSIS / GOOD POINTS

High in dietary fiber, High in niacin, High in phosphorus, High in potassium, High in riboflavin, Very high in selenium, Very high in thiamin, High in vitamin A, Very high vitamin B6, Very high in vitamin C

PO' BOY PORK RAMON SKILLET

Don't know what to do with all those ramen noodles in your dorm room. This recipe pairs ramen noodles, with the flavors of pork and fresh stir-fried veggies, so well that you won't realize that you are still living on a budget.

Prep Time: 10 Minutes
Cook Time: 10 Minutes
Servings: 4

INGREDIENTS

¾ pound pork tenderloin, cut into 1/8-inch strips
6 ounces egg noodles
1 ½ cups water
1 medium red bell pepper, cut into 3/4 inch pieces (1 cup)

1 cup broccoli (flowerets)
4 medium green onions, cut into 1-inch pieces (1/2 cup)
1 tbsp. parsley (chopped fresh or 2 teaspoons parsley flakes, if desired)
1 tablespoon soy sauce

DIRECTIONS

> Add pork to a non-stick skillet and cook for 6 minutes or till cooked stirring occasionally.
> Add broken noodles, and rest of ingredients into the skillet.
> Bring to a boil and add only 1 packet of the roman seasoning to the electric skillet and cook for 5 minutes.
> Garnish and serve.

NUTRITIONAL FACTS:

Serving Size 289 g, Amount Per Serving, Calories 205Calories from Fat 37, Total Fat 4.1g, Saturated Fat 1.2g, Trans Fat 0.0g, Cholesterol 74mg, Sodium 290mg, Potassium 565mg, Total Carbohydrates 15.5g, Dietary Fiber 2.2g, Sugars 2.2g, Protein 25.7g

Vitamin A 26%, Vitamin C 104%, Calcium 4%, Iron 11%, Nutrition Grade A, Based on a 2000 calorie diet

NUTRITIONAL ANALYSIS / GOOD POINTS

High in niacin, High in phosphorus, High in riboflavin, Very high in selenium, Very high in thiamin, High in vitamin A, High in vitamin B6, Very high in vitamin C

HEARTY ONE-POT SAUSAGE & BROCCOLI SCALLOPED POTATOES

Only one piece of kitchenware is needed for this delicious dish. Your parents always told you to eat your broccoli, and you are, but there are pleasing additions like potatoes, salsa, and sausage to go along with the famed vegetable. This entrée is very easy to prepare and in the end, you have a complete meal to share with the family or friends!

Prep Time: 10 Minutes
Cook Time: 30 Minutes
Servings: 6

INGREDIENTS

5 oz. scalloped potatoes (1 box)
2 cups hot water
2/3 cup milk
2 tablespoons margarine or butter
1lb Kielbasa sausage (sliced fully cooked from 1-lb ring)

½ cup salsa (any variety)
2 cups broccoli (frozen florets)
4 cloves garlic, minced
1 tablespoon chives
1/3 cup grated cheddar cheese

DIRECTIONS

> In a skillet or electric skillet, bring to a boil the potatoes, sauce mix, hot water, milk, margarine, garlic, and chives, stirring occasionally the mixture.
> Mix in the sausage and salsa then lower the heat. Simmer for 15-20 minutes with the electric skillet covered, stirring every so often. You should see the sauce thicken a little more as it's cooking.
> Add the cheese and broccoli and stir. Re-cover and cook for 6-8 minutes. The sauce should richen up even more upon cooking and the vegetables cook to their right texture.

NUTRITIONAL FACTS:

Serving Size 336 g, Amount Per Serving, Calories 407, Calories from Fat 255, Total Fat 28.4g, Saturated Fat 9.4g, Trans Fat 0.2g, Cholesterol 73mg, Sodium 816mg34%, Potassium 732mg21%, Total Carbohydrates 18.0g, Dietary Fiber 3.0g, Sugars 3.9g, Protein 20.2g

Vitamin A 11%, Vitamin C 73%, Calcium 14%, Iron 10%, Nutrition Grade B-, Based on a 2000 calorie diet

NUTRITIONAL ANALYSIS / GOOD POINTS

High in vitamin B6, High in vitamin C

FRESH AND TENDER "ISLAND THYME" PORK

Though most fantasize about spending time on the beach, drinking fruity cocktails, and eating juicy and fresh cuisine, it is possible to have an island meal at home. The pineapple, apricot, and orange seep into the meat, and the curry cures your island fever. This course has all the right spices, especially the sprinkle of thyme that brings the whole meal together in the end!

Prep Time: 30 Minutes
Cook Time: 15 Minutes
Servings: 4

INGREDIENTS

2 tablespoons pineapple jam (preserves)
1 tablespoon orange marmalade
3 tablespoons orange juice, plus more if needed
1/2 teaspoon minced fresh ginger
1/2 teaspoon curry powder
3.5 oz. pineapple rings (4 fresh rings or canned 1/2-inch-thick, cut in half, any juice reserved)

2 teaspoons butter
4 5-ounce pork loin chops (boneless 1/2 inch thick), trimmed
2 tablespoons chopped fresh thyme, divided
1/2 teaspoon salt, divided
1/4 teaspoon freshly ground pepper, divided

1 oz. cilantro

DIRECTIONS

› Mix the pineapple reserves, orange marmalade, 3 tablespoons ginger, orange juice, and curry powder and set aside until needed. Also...set aside enough orange juice to the pineapple juice...orange juice should be about 1/3 cup total...

› Melt butter in a large nonstick skillet over medium-high heat. Season the pork chops with 1/4 teaspoon salt, 1/8 teaspoon pepper and about 1/2 tablespoon thyme, on each side then add to skillet. Cook on one side for a few minutes then turn on other side after you see them brown.

› Lower the heat on the stove (around medium) and add the rest of the juice you put to the side. Cook the chops for a few minutes before move over to a clean plate; cover with foil.

› Using the same electric skillet, cook pineapple, reserved sauce and the rest of the thyme for only a minute or two.

› Cover the pork and pineapple with however much sauce you desire; garnish with cilantro. (Can also garnish with parsley for cilantro substitute, if desired)

NUTRITIONAL FACTS:

Serving Size 205 g, Amount Per Serving, Calories 535, Calories from Fat 336, Total Fat 37.4g, Saturated Fat 14.5g, Trans Fat 0.0g, Cholesterol 127mg, Sodium 414mg, Potassium 605mg, Total Carbohydrates 16.2g, Dietary Fiber 1.4g, Sugars 11.4g, Protein 32.5g

Vitamin A 12%, Vitamin C 44%, Calcium 8%, Iron 20%, Nutrition Grade B-, Based on a 2000 calorie diet

NUTRITIONAL ANALYSIS / GOOD POINTS

High in selenium, High in thiamin

BROILED AND BRAISED TENDERLOIN
WITH FRESH MANGO SALSA

There's just something about pork and fruit that goes well together. The juices of both complement each other, and it's very apparent in this Caribbean-influenced entrée. Mango and lime add citrus to the spices and the tenderloin is cooked to be just as juicy as its marinade. A light and quick dinner for a breezy summer evening!

Prep Time: 10 Minutes
Cook Time: 25 Minutes
Servings: 4

INGREDIENTS

1 mango, chopped
2 scallions, chopped
1 tablespoon plus 1 teaspoon oil
1 lime, zest and juice
1/2 lemon, zest and juice

1/4 teaspoon crushed red pepper
Kosher salt
1 1/4 pounds pork tenderloin 1 tenderloin)
1 teaspoon ground coriander

DIRECTIONS

〉 Mix together 1 tablespoon of the oil, mango, scallions, lime zest and juice, lemon zest and juice, crushed red pepper, and a pinch of salt then put this mixture to the side and save for later.

〉 Over the meat put a teaspoon of oil and spread around the meat. After that you will season with coriander and a couple pinches of teaspoon of salt.

〉 Broil for 6-7 minutes on each side. Make sure you check the meat to see if it is browning before you turn it over to its other. Repeat the process.

〉 Give the meat about 5 minutes to cool before slicing, and serve with the salsa mixture.

〉 Delicious recipe that is simple and a ton of flavor.

NUTRITIONAL FACTS:

Serving Size 77 g, Amount Per Serving, Calories 82, Calories from Fat 43, Total Fat 4.7g, Saturated Fat 0.6, Trans Fat 0.0g, Cholesterol 0mg, Sodium 41mg, Potassium 121mg, Total Carbohydrates 10.4g, Dietary Fiber 1.5g. Sugars 8.0g, Protein 0.6g

Vitamin A 10%, Vitamin C 39%, Calcium 1%, Iron 2%, Nutrition Grade B, Based on a 2000 calorie diet

NUTRITIONAL ANALYSIS / GOOD POINTS

NUTRITIONAL ANALYSIS / GOOD POINTS

No cholesterol, Low in sodium, High in vitamin A, Very high in vitamin C

SIZZLING & SPICY HONEY JALAPENO SPINACH PORK

These pork wraps are a multipurpose dish; they can either be served as an appetizer or a main course, depending on how hungry you are! The chili paste and jalapeno add plenty of spice, and with the addition of spinach, the dish becomes healthier without losing any of the great flavors within the stir-fry. A win-win!

Prep Time: 30 Minutes
Cook Time: 15 Minutes
Servings: 4

INGREDIENTS

3/4 lb. boneless pork loin, cut into
1/4" by 2" strips
1/2 large red pepper, cut into strips
1/2 cup fresh bean spouts
1/3 cup fresh leek strips
1 large jalapeño pepper, trimmed,
seeded and diced

1 Tbsp. hot chili paste with garlic
1 teaspoon cayenne pepper
1 Tbsp. rice wine vinegar
4 Tbsp. soy sauce
1 Tbsp. honey
1 cup baby spinach
1/3 cup peanuts, chopped (optional)

DIRECTIONS

> Set washed spinach on a serving plate either as a bed or around the side.

> Except for the spinach and peanuts, combine all the ingredients in a bowl, or mixing container. Refrigerate so the meat can marinate for about an hour. (You can marinade longer to have the juices set in the meat even deeper)

> When you're ready to start cooking, remove the bowl and sit it out for approximately 15 minutes or till the meat is at room temperature.

> Add ingredients to a preheated electric skillet on medium-high heat preferably. The meat is done when it has started to brown, but cook to desired doneness. (The longer you cook the browner it will become) Then add the meat on the of spinach. If you wish you can sprinkle and garnish the dish with chopped nuts. (Add a parsley garnish if desired as well for an extra color to the dish.)

NUTRITION FACTS

Serving Size 165 g, Amount Per Serving, Calories 245, Calories from Fat 88, Total Fat 9.8g, Saturated Fat 1.9g, Trans Fat 0.0g, Cholesterol 63mg,

Sodium 1006mg. Potassium 596mg, Total Carbohydrates 12.0g, Dietary Fiber 2.1g, Sugars 7.4g, Protein 27.3g

Vitamin A 40%, Vitamin C 52%, Calcium 4%, Iron 14%, Nutrition Grade A, Based on a 2000 calorie diet

NUTRITIONAL ANALYSIS / GOOD POINTS

High in niacin, High in phosphorus, Very high in selenium, Very high in thiamin, High in vitamin A, High in vitamin B6, Very high in vitamin C

CHAPTER 13:
MISC.: SOUPS

Nothing beats a bowl of warm delicious homemade soup...especially with some amazing accessories to dip or crumble up in with it! Just like grandma used to make, straight from "your very own kitchen!" Yummy, tasty, delightful and "snuggly delicious"...enjoy!

GOOEY GRILLED CHEESE MINIS IN CREAMY TOMATO SOUP

What is the go-to meal when you can't think of anything and are short on food? Grilled cheese, of course. Imagine preparing for the delicious backup plan now. A simple dish can be altered to something amazing with a little patience and preparation. Plus, when will there be a better time to make small grilled cheese sandwiches floating atop tomato soup? Probably all the time.

Prep Time: 10 Minutes
Cook Time: 40 Minutes
Servings: 6

INGREDIENTS

3 tablespoons olive oil
2 yellow onions, chopped
3 cloves garlic (minced)
4 cups chicken stock
1 (28-ounce) can crushed tomatoes
1 tablespoon oregano
1 tablespoon basil
2 tablespoon sea salt
1 teaspoon Freshly ground black pepper

1/2 cup orzo
1/2 cup heavy cream

Grilled Cheese Croutons:
5 oz. wheat bread (4 slices country wheat)
2 tablespoons unsalted butter, melted
4 ounces cheddar cheese, grated

DIRECTIONS

> Add olive oil to a large electric skillet and heat on about medium for a couple of minutes. Lower the heat just a tad and cook the onions for 12-14 and keep stirring till it starts to brown in the electric skillet, then mix in the garlic

> Cook this for an additional minute. After the garlic and onion have cooked, add the chicken stock, tomatoes, oregano, basil, 1 tablespoon salt and 1 teaspoon pepper and stir till the soup starts to boil. Cook on low for about 12-14 minutes after lowering the heat.

> While this is taking place, boil water and a few pinches of salt in another skillet. Cook the orzo for 5-6 minutes, drain, and add to the soup (Don't worry about the orzo being done when you drain it...while it is cooking in the soup it will finish cooking). Add cream stirring occasionally and cook the soup for about 7-9 minutes. (Make sure you keep stirring the soup while it is cooking)

GRILLED CHEESE CROUTONS DIRECTIONS

> Place the four slices of buttered bread in the electric skillet, buttered side down. Pile cheddar on two of the slices and the place the others on top of the cheese, buttered side up. Grill for just a couple of minutes each side, flipping the sandwiches halfway. (Make sure not to burn the bread)
> After letting sit for 1 minutes, cut the grilled cheese up into little squares and let the squares float on top of the soup.

NUTRITIONAL FACTS:

Serving Size 419 g, Amount Per Serving, Calories 396, Calories from Fat 201, Total Fat 22.4g, Saturated Fat 10.0g, Trans Fat 0.2g, Cholesterol 44mg, Sodium 2897mg121%, Potassium 173mg, Total Carbohydrates 36.6g, Dietary Fiber 7.6g, Sugars 11.7g, Protein 14.1g

Vitamin A 37%, Vitamin C 22%, Calcium 27%, Iron 20%, Nutrition Grade C+, Based on a 2000 calorie diet

JAMBALAYA FOR JOY

We look towards the Bayou for this classic Creole dish. The wonderful thing about Jambalaya is that there are thousands of variations and depending on the person, every one of them is enjoyable! It is a one-pot mixture of essentials: meat, vegetables, and grains. This dish is a meal in its own that everyone can be satisfied with.

Prep Time: 20 Minutes
Cook Time: 1 Hour
Servings: 6

INGREDIENTS

1 lb. chicken breasts, cut into bite-size pieces
1 lb. sausage, cut into ¼-inch thick slices
1/4 tbsp. olive oil
1/2 c. onion, chopped
1/2 c shallots
1 large bell pepper, chopped
2 cloves of garlic, minced

1 - 14.5 oz. can diced tomatoes (do not drain)
1 1/2 c. chicken stock
1 c rice
1/2 tsp. dried thyme
1 tbsp. parsley
1 tsp. paprika
1 tsp. chili powder

DIRECTIONS

> Add olive oil to an electric skillet over medium heat and then place the sausage and chicken until the chicken is done.
> Remove the meat from the electric skillet, and then add the onion, shallot, bell pepper and garlic; cook this sizzling mixture until onion is tender, adding the chicken broth, diced tomatoes, thyme, paprika, chili powder, parsley, and bay leaves. (You can add a teaspoon of crushed red peppers to heat things up just a bit)
> Lower the heat and cover cooking for approximately 18-20 minutes.
> Mix in rice and the meat that had been set aside. Make heat into a slow boil and cover for another 18-20 minutes.
> Season to taste with a little salt and pepper. (You can keep the bay leaf in to keep the flavor going)

NUTRITIONAL FACTS:

Serving Size 301 g, Amount Per Serving, Calories 547, Calories from Fat 254, Total Fat 28.2g, Saturated Fat 8.6g, Trans Fat 0.2g, Cholesterol 131mg, Sodium 842mg, Potassium 586mg, Total Carbohydrates 30.7g, Dietary Fiber 1.6g, Sugars 2.0g, Protein 39.9g

Vitamin A 29%, Vitamin C 65%, Calcium 5%, Iron 22%. Nutrition Grade B-, Based on a 2000 calorie diet

NUTRITIONAL ANALYSIS / GOOD POINTS
Low in sugar, High in niacin, High in vitamin C

CHAPTER 14:
VEGGIES AND SIDES:

We.....this one is for you non meat eaters out there! We've created a larger section of this book "just for you!" You will enjoy all of the mouthwatering, succulent and flavorful varieties of yummy foods we have put together for you in this chapter. Write us a review and let us know which is your favorite! And remember what mom used to say..."Don't forget your veggies!" ...Enjoy!

SWEET AND SAVORY POTATO PIZZA

Eggs and sweet potato in a pizza you ask? It can be done and with pizza

Prep Time: 20 Minutes
Cook Time: 20 Minutes
Servings: 4

INGREDIENTS

6 eggs
1 cup half-and-half
1 tsp. kosher salt
½ tsp. freshly ground pepper
2 cups sweet potatoes

2 cups kale (firmly packed chopped)
½ small red onion
2 cloves garlic
3 oz. goat cheese

DIRECTIONS

> Prepare eggs: whisk eggs, salt and pepper and half-and- half in a mixing bowl.
> In a non-stick skillet cook the sweet potatoes for 10 minutes. (lightly oil if desired)
> Transfer to a plate.
> Add the kale, onions and garlic until kale is cooked. Approximately 4 minutes.
> Put in potatoes and egg mixture for 3 more minutes.
> Add cheese on top showering all over and bake at 345 degrees for 12 minutes.
> Depending on the size of your oven it may take just a couple minutes longer.
> Garnish and serve.

NUTRITIONAL FACTS:

Serving Size 268 g, Amount Per Serving, Calories 381, Calories from Fat 191, Total Fat 21.2g, Saturated Fat 11.6g, Trans Fat 0.0g, Cholesterol 290mg, Sodium 794mg, Potassium 976mg, Total Carbohydrates 29.5g, Dietary Fiber 3.9g, Sugars 1.8g, Protein 19.0g, Vitamin A 123%, Vitamin C 91%, Calcium 35%, Iron 15%, Nutrition Grade B+, Based on a 2000 calorie diet

NUTRITIONAL ANALYSIS / GOOD POINTS

Low in sugar, High in phosphorus, High in selenium, Very high in vitamin A, Very high in vitamin C

SQUASH AND GARLIC EGGPLANT LASAGNA–

This recipe will blow you away. Not only are you making lasagna in a skillet, but you are making it without noodles and you won't even be able to tell the difference.

Prep Time: 35 Minutes
Cook Time: 35 Minutes
Servings: 6

INGREDIENTS

1 peeled and chopped eggplant
1 chopped zucchini
1 dice yellow squash
3 chopped cloves garlic

1 cup ricotta cheese
3 tbsp. grated parmesan cheese
1 cup traditional pasta sauce
1 cup shredded mozzarella cheese

DIRECTIONS

> In a non-stick skillet, add and cook the eggplant, zucchini and squash for 10 minutes.
> Add the garlic and cook for 5 more minutes stirring occasionally. Remove vegetables and keep warm.
> Combine ricotta and parmesan in skillet with pasta sauce.
> Add the cooked vegetable mixture, cover and cook for 20 minutes.
> Let it cool...garnish and serve.

NUTRITIONAL FACTS:

Serving Size 250 g, Amount Per Serving, Calories 197, Calories from Fat 86, Total Fat 9.6g, Saturated Fat 5.3g, Trans Fat 0.0g, Cholesterol 29mg, Sodium 373mg, Potassium 540mg, Total Carbohydrates 15.8g, Dietary Fiber 4.5g, Sugars 7.3g, Protein 13.6g

Vitamin A 13%, Vitamin C 23%, Calcium 31%, Iron 5%, Nutrition Grade A, Based on a 2000 calorie diet

NUTRITIONAL ANALYSIS / GOOD POINTS

High in calcium, High in phosphorus, High in vitamin C

CALIFORNIA MEATLESS CILANTRO QUESADILLAS

These easy to make "bursting with flavor" quesadillas take less than 20 minutes to make. This is a perfect recipe for when you want to be healthy but don't have a lot of time to make dinner.

Prep Time: 15 Minutes
Cook Time: 15 Minutes
Servings: 4

INGREDIENTS

16oz black beans (can substitute with pinto beans)
½ cup shredded Monterey jack cheese
½ cup fresh salsa

4 whole-wheat tortillas (at least 8")
1 ripe diced avocado
¼ cup cilantro

DIRECTIONS

> Preparing Quesadillas: Cut up the cilantro very fine!
> Mix the cilantro beans, cheese and salsa in a mixing container.
> Combine mixture into a tortilla, spread evenly and fold. Continue each until all mixture has been used.
> in a non-stick skillet add two quesadillas and cook for two minutes on both sides. (You will see the tortillas start to brown)
> Repeat.
> Garnish with avocado, and salsa and serve.

NUTRITIONAL FACTS:

Serving Size 235 g, Amount Per Serving, Calories 603, Calories from Fat 148, Total Fat 16.4g, Saturated Fat 5.3g, Trans Fat 0.0g, Cholesterol 13mg, Sodium 291mg, Potassium 2083mg, Total Carbohydrates 87.9g, Dietary Fiber 22.7g, Sugars 3.9g, Protein 30.8g

Vitamin A 7%, Vitamin C 10%, Calcium 28%, Iron 36%, Nutrition Grade A, Based on a 2000 calorie diet

NUTRITIONAL ANALYSIS / GOOD POINTS

Very low in cholesterol, Low in sodium, Low in sugar, High in dietary fiber, High in thiamin

FIRE ROASTED SIZZLING ZUCCHINI
AND RICE RECIPE

Fresh Zucchini never tasted so good! When combined with this rich and healthy dish, these fire roasted tomatoes, beans and rice give you the ultimate flavor for your taste buds in an a simple and easy to cook meal!

This flavorful and hearty Zucchini dish is a quick prep dish that will make you look like you slaved in the kitchen for hours. This is an amazing dish to impress your peers. They will think you had this dish prepared by a professional chef! Simple, quick and will have your taste buds screaming for more!

Prep Time: 25 Minutes
Cook Time: 25 Minutes
Servings: 4

INGREDIENTS

1 chopped zucchini
tablespoon of butter
½ cup chopped green bell pepper
16 oz. black beans (whole 1 can)
14 oz. tomatoes (1 can diced fire roasted)

¾ cup chicken broth
1 cup uncooked instant white rice
½ cup shredded cheese (cheddar and Monterey jack cheese blend)

DIRECTIONS

> In a non-stick skillet heat a tablespoon of butter, then add zucchini and cook for 5 minutes.
> Then add the mixture of beans, tomatoes and water and cook for about 3 min.
> After this starts to boil...add rice, cover and simmer for 7 minutes.
> Garnish with cheese and serve.

NUTRITIONAL FACTS:

Serving Size 288 g, Amount Per Serving, Calories 477, Calories from Fat 72, Total Fat 8.0g, Saturated Fat 4.3g, Cholesterol 18mg, Sodium 216mg, Potassium 1703mg, Total Carbohydrates 77.4g, Dietary Fiber 15.7g, Sugars 5.2g, Protein 25.9g

Vitamin A 24%, Vitamin C 49%, Calcium 21%, Iron 35%, Nutrition Grade A, Based on a 2000 calorie diet

NUTRITIONAL ANALYSIS / GOOD POINTS

Low in cholesterol, Low in sodium, High in dietary fiber, High in thiamin

CHEESEY SPINACH & GARLIC ARTICOKE SKILLET DIP

A little something to dip your chips, veggies, crackers or crusted bread till your hearts content! This one is a sure winner for that pot luck or gathering with friends! This dip is a sure winner and party favorite and will make you look like a pro!

Prep Time: 25 Minutes
Cook Time: 25 Minutes
Servings: 4

INGREDIENTS

2 ½ cups fresh baby spinach
3 cloves chopped garlic
1 cup ricotta cheese
1 package cream cheese

1 ½ cups chopped artichoke hearts
1 cup shredded provolone cheese
1 roasted red pepper (garnish)

DIRECTIONS

> In a non-stick skillet add minced garlic, and baby spinach. Cook for 5 minutes stirring on occasion.
> Turn off heat and stir in cheeses.
> Add the mixture with artichoke hearts and the red pepper to the skillet, with a layer of cheese.
> (You can add a little salt and fresh ground pepper just for flavor)
> Bake for 400 for 6 minutes.
> Garnish with some of the leftover red peppers and serve.
> "Great for dipping with buttered with crackers" Be creative with what you dip this dish!

NUTRITIONAL FACTS:

Serving Size 204 g, Amount Per Serving, Calories 311, Calories from Fat 192, Total Fat 21.3g, Saturated Fat 13.4g, Trans Fat 0.0g, Cholesterol 65mg, Sodium 533mg, Potassium 470mg, Total Carbohydrates 12.1g, Dietary Fiber 3.3g, Sugars 1.8g, Protein 19.5g

Vitamin A 62%, Vitamin C 71%, Calcium 48%, Iron 11%, Nutrition Grade B, Based on a 2000 calorie diet

NUTRITIONAL ANALYSIS / GOOD POINTS

Low in sugar, High in calcium, High in phosphorus, High in vitamin A, Very high in vitamin C

MIXED VEGTABLE RELISH–

When you just want vegetables. This mixed vegetable relish will satisfy your hunger cravings in under 30 minutes.

Prep Time: 25 Minutes
Cook Time: 25 Minutes
Servings: 10

INGREDIENTS

1 large diced white onion
18 ounces' zucchini (chopped medium)
1 large chopped red bell pepper
1 large chopped orange bell pepper
1 10-ounce package frozen lima beans or shelled edamame

1 10-ounce package frozen corn kernels
1 tsp. minced fresh marjoram
1 tablespoon oregano
teaspoon fresh ground pepper
1 tsp. Sea salt

DIRECTIONS -

> In a non-stick skillet combine onions, zucchini, peppers, lima beans and corn and cook for 10 minutes.
> Add marjoram, oregano, sea salt and fresh ground pepper and cook for another 5 minutes.
> Garnish and serve.

NUTRITIONAL FACTS:

Serving Size 157 g, Amount Per Serving, Calories 81, Calories from Fat 6, Total Fat 0.7g, Cholesterol 0mg, Sodium 197mg, Potassium 434mg, Total Carbohydrates 16.7g, Dietary Fiber 3.9g, Sugars 4.2g, Protein 3.8g

Vitamin A 26%, Vitamin C 99%, Calcium 3%, Iron 9%, Nutrition Grade A, Based on a 2000 calorie diet

NUTRITIONAL ANALYSIS / GOOD POINTS

Very low in saturated fat, No cholesterol, High in dietary fiber, High in iron, Very high in manganese, High in magnesium, High in phosphorus, High in potassium, Very high in vitamin A, Very high in vitamin B6, Very high in vitamin C

THE TASTE OF SPRING IN A SKILLET

Spring is in the air and what better way to celebrate the season then by adding it to your plate. This is a recipe that brings all the beauty of spring right into your kitchen.

Prep Time: 15 Minutes
Cook Time: 15 Minutes
Servings: 4

INGREDIENTS

16 baby carrots (peeled and chopped with tops)
¾ tsp. kosher salt
12 ounces' sugar snap peas

1 tbsp. chopped fresh tarragon
¼ tbsp. freshly ground black pepper
1 tbsp. grated lemon rind
1 tsp. fresh lemon juice

DIRECTIONS -

- Prepare vegetables: Cut all vegetables to your liking.
- bring water, carrots and peas to a boil in a non-stick electric skillet for only a few minutes until soft but firm. Then disregard water.
- In a non-stick skillet combine vegetables, seasoning, rind and lemon juice, cook for 2 minutes.
- Garnish and serve.

NUTRITIONAL FACTS:
Serving Size 132 g, Amount Per Serving, Calories 53, Calories from Fat 3, Total Fat 0.3g, Cholesterol 0mg, Sodium 473mg, Potassium 290mg, Total Carbohydrates 10.5g, Dietary Fiber 3.6g, Sugars 5.4g, Protein 2.8g

Vitamin A 129%, Vitamin C 91%, Calcium 6%, Iron 13%, Nutrition Grade A, Based on a 2000 calorie diet

NUTRITIONAL ANALYSIS / GOOD POINTS

Very low in saturated fat, No cholesterol, High in calcium, Very high in dietary fiber, Very high in iron, Very high in manganese, High in magnesium, High, High in phosphorus, High in potassium, High in thiamin, Very high in vitamin A, High in vitamin B6, Very high in vitamin C

COATED ASPARAGUS WITH RIPE AVACADO

Asparagus and Avocado are great additions to any meal, so why not put them together in the same dish? There is no reason not to outside of an allergy of course. Plenty of other vegetables make this a colorful salad full of freshness and flavor!

Prep Time: 20 Minutes
Cook Time: 23 Minutes
Servings: 4

INGREDIENTS

1 1/2 pounds' fresh asparagus
1/2 cup olive oil, divided
1 1/2 tablespoons chopped fresh basil, divided
1/2 teaspoon lemon pepper
1/2 teaspoon salt, divided
1/4 cup balsamic vinegar
1 garlic clove, minced
1 cup halved cherry tomatoes (about 1/2 pt.)

1/2 cup chopped red bell pepper
1/8 cup finely chopped red onion
1/8 cup finely chopped sweet yellow onion
1 head Bibb lettuce, torn into bite-size pieces
1 avocado, sliced
Parsley for garnish

DIRECTIONS

> Cut off the ends of asparagus and dispose of.
> In a mixing container, add 1 Tbsp. olive oil, 1 ½ teaspoon basil, lemon pepper, and 1/4 tsp. salt.
> Get a brush & coat (lightly brush) asparagus with olive oil mixture, and place in skillet.
> Bake for 10 to 12 minutes, then let the asparagus sit and cool for 8-10 minutes.
> Take the balsamic vinegar, garlic, and remaining olive oil, basil, and salt...stirring and mixing it all together.
> Combine tomatoes, bell pepper, onion, and 1 Tbsp. balsamic vinegar mixture and toss.
> Put the tomato mixture and asparagus over some lettuce on each plate, slice an avocado and divide, and with a brush...brush the rest of the balsamic mix to your liking.

NUTRITIONAL FACTS:

Serving Size 410 g, Amount Per Serving, Calories 383, Calories from Fat 319, Total Fat 35.5g, Saturated Fat 5.7g, Trans Fat 0.0g, Cholesterol 0mg, Sodium 306mg, Potassium 863mg, Total Carbohydrates 17.1g, Dietary Fiber 8.5g, Sugars 6.3g, Protein 5.8g

Vitamin A 43%, Vitamin C 67%, Calcium 6%, Iron 36%, Nutrition Grade B+, Based on a 2000 calorie diet

NUTRITIONAL ANALYSIS / GOOD POINTS

No cholesterol, High in vitamin A, High in vitamin B6, High in vitamin C

SIMMERING BARLEY PARMESEAN

Barley is one of the healthiest side dishes because it contains protein, fiber, and is considered a whole grain. In addition, it is not short on flavor! The barley mixes well with the tomatoes and cheese providing a side dish that is gratifying enough to be its own meal. Beer is still an option as a side to this side.

Prep Time: 10 Minutes
Cook Time: 30 Minutes
Servings: 4

INGREDIENTS

2 tablespoons olive oil
1 onion, finely chopped
1/2 teaspoon salt
1/4 teaspoon pepper
2 cups quick-cook barley
1 can (28 oz.) diced tomatoes, drained
1 cup dry white wine

2 1/2 cups water
8 cups mustard green leaves or spinach, torn into pieces
2 ounces Brie (rind removed), cut into small pieces
1/2 cup grated Parmesan (2 oz.)
1/4 cup chopped Oregano

DIRECTIONS

› Add oil to an electric skillet over medium heat. Cook the onion with salt and pepper, and stir occasionally for 5-7 minutes.
› Mix in the barley, tomatoes, wine and water and increase heat, bringing the ingredients to a simmering boil.
› Lower the heat keeping the simmer for 10-12 minutes while continuing to stir the barley in the electric skillet.
› Mix in the mustard greens, Brie, oregano, and ¼ cup of the Cheese and cook an additional several minutes while stirring making it nice and creamy.
› Divide and shower the servings with what is left of the Parmesan.
› Delicious...

NUTRITIONAL FACTS

Serving Size 612 g, Amount Per Serving, Calories 566, Calories from Fat 134, Total Fat 14.9g, Saturated Fat 4.6g, Trans Fat 0.0g, Cholesterol 15mg, Sodium 456mg, Potassium 1412mg, Total Carbohydrates 84.8g, Dietary Fiber 22.2g, Sugars 8.1g, Protein 19.3g

Vitamin A 155%, Vitamin C 80%, Calcium 30%, Iron 44%, Nutrition Grade B+, Based on a 2000 calorie diet

NUTRITIONAL ANALYSIS / GOOD POINTS

Low in cholesterol, High in dietary fiber, High in manganese, High in selenium, Very high in vitamin A, High in vitamin C

FRESH AND FLAVORFUL CAPRESE PASTA

A vegetarian's delight! This Caprese pasta salad is light and fresh and will add flavor to any main course. It's quick, easy, and satisfying. There's nothing more you can ask for. The tomatoes and mozzarella mixed with the basil offers a true Italian taste wherever you're dining.

Prep Time: 5 Minutes
Cook Time: 10 Minutes
Servings: 4

INGREDIENTS

6 ounces' whole grain fusilli or rotini pasta
⅓ cup olive oil
2 cloves minced garlic
2 pints' cherry or grape tomatoes
½ teaspoon sea salt

8 ounces' baby mozzarella balls (ciliegine)
2 tablespoons chopped Basil
2 tablespoons chopped Oregano
2 to 3 teaspoons white balsamic vinegar, to taste

DIRECTIONS

> Boil the pasta in a large pot of water (always add a little salt to boil faster and for a little flavor), drain, then use the same pot to set aside the pasta.

> Meanwhile, add olive oil to an electric skillet over low to medium heat. (Do not cook the olive oil on too high because it can burn at high temperatures) Cook the tomatoes, garlic, and ½ teaspoon sea salt with the cover on. Make sure to check occasionally but keep mixing anywhere from 6-7 minutes. Put everything into the pasta and mix it all in nicely.

> Slice the mozzarella balls in half and add to the mixture along with oregano and basil. The vinegar can be added but make sure you add Just a little for flavoring. (Vinegar can be strong so add moderately)

NUTRITIONAL FACTS:

Serving Size 224 g, Amount Per Serving, Calories 368, Calories from Fat 104, Total Fat 11.6g. Saturated Fat 6.3g, Trans Fat 0.0g, Cholesterol 61mg, Sodium 590mg, Potassium 385mg, Total Carbohydrates 46.0g, Dietary Fiber 3.5g, Sugars 15.1g, Protein 22.6g

Vitamin A 15%, Vitamin C 17%, Calcium 47%, Iron 16%, Nutrition Grade B, Based on a 2000 calorie diet

NUTRITIONAL ANALYSIS / GOOD POINTS
High in calcium, High in phosphorus

POTENT STUFFED PARMESAN PORTEBELLO GRATIN

The beauty of mushrooms is that they can be cooked in different ways, cooked with different things, and serve as a side to most dishes. A very useful vegetable! Of course, bread crumbs and cheese would go well with mushrooms. Add herbs to the filling and you have a deliciously awesome dish.

Prep Time: 15 Minutes
Cook Time: 35 Minutes
Servings: 6

INGREDIENTS

2 tablespoons olive oil, plus more for baking sheet
6 Portobello mushrooms, stems removed and reserved
1/4 cup finely grated Parmesan cheese (1 ounce)
1/4 cup plain dry breadcrumbs
3 tablespoons finely chopped fresh flat-leaf parsley

3 tablespoons chopped fresh chives
2 shallots, thinly sliced
1 pound white or cremini mushrooms, sliced
1/2 cup dry white wine
1/2 cup heavy cream
1 teaspoon coarse salt
1/4 teaspoon freshly ground pepper
1/4 teaspoon red pepper flakes

DIRECTIONS

> Place the Portobello caps with their gill sides down and lightly brush oil in the bottom of the skillet. Cook at 350 degrees for about 20 minutes then let cool. (The mushrooms should be tender by this time)

> In a mixing container, mix together cheese, breadcrumbs, 1 tablespoon parsley, 1 tablespoon chives, and 1 tablespoon oil.

> Dice up the mushroom stems. Add the remaining oil to a skillet and cook these over medium to low heat. Cook the shallots and make sure you keep mixing while cooking for 2-4 minutes then mix in the mushrooms and the diced stems, cooking and mixing for an additional 5 minutes. The wine can then be added, and then after 2 more minutes and stir in cream. The remainder of both the parsley and chives, and the salt and red and black pepper. After everything is combined, turn off the heat and remove the electric skillet from the burner. (Doing this keeps the dish from cooking too long)

> Place the mushroom caps on a clean baking sheet with their gills facing up. Evenly spread the mixture and crumbs atop each cap. Broil for 2 minutes. (You will notice them getting a nice crisp brown...then they're done!) Fast...Fun Dish for Everyone to Enjoy!

NUTRITIONAL FACTS:

Serving Size 227 g, Amount Per Serving, Calories 240, Calories from Fat 140, Total Fat 15.5g. Saturated Fat 6.0g, Cholesterol 28mg, Sodium 592mg, Potassium 728mg, Total Carbohydrates 14.5g, Dietary Fiber 1.5g, Sugars 3.2g, Protein 7.2g

Vitamin A 17%, Vitamin C 12%, Calcium 11%, Iron 12%, Nutrition Grade C+, Based on a 2000 calorie diet

NUTRITIONAL ANALYSIS / GOOD POINTS

High in niacin, High in riboflavin, Very high in selenium, Very high in vitamin B6

SAUTEED VEGGIES ATOP A BED OF SPICY QUINOA

Kee-noo-ah. The name isn't why the grain is great, but is the most complex part of this side dish. Quinoa is a very healthy alternative to already-healthy foods like rice, and is gradually becoming part of the Superfood category. The black beans, spices, and corn give the grain a Mexican kick in this sure-to-please healthy side dish!

Prep Time: 15 Minutes
Cook Time: 35 Minutes
Servings: 6

INGREDIENTS

1 teaspoon ground cumin
1 1/2 cups vegetable broth
3/4 cup quinoa
3 cloves garlic, chopped
1 onion, chopped
1 teaspoon vegetable oil
1/2 cup chopped fresh cilantro

2 (15 ounce) cans black beans, rinsed and drained
1 cup frozen corn kernels
salt and ground black pepper to taste
1/4 teaspoon cayenne pepper
1/4 teaspoon paprika
1/4 teaspoon basil

DIRECTIONS

> Add oil to an electric skillet over medium heat and cook the onion and garlic for about 7-8 minutes while occasionally stirring.
> Place quinoa into the onions and garlic, smothering the mixture with vegetable broth. Sprinkle the seasonings, except for the cilantro and bring everything to a boil. Lower the heat and cover the electric skillet, letting the ingredients cook for approximate 15-18 minutes.
> While it remains simmering, put in the corn and cook for about 5 minutes. Lastly, add the cilantro and black beans.
> If you've never had Quinoa…you will be a believer of this dish! :)

NUTRITIONAL FACTS:

Serving Size 274 g, Amount Per Serving, Calories 613, Calories from Fat 43, Total Fat 4.7g, Saturated Fat 1.0g, Cholesterol 0mg, Sodium 589mg, Potassium 2391mg, Total Carbohydrates 110.3g, Dietary Fiber 24.3g, Sugars 4.9g, Protein 36.0g

Vitamin A 5%, Vitamin C 6%, Calcium 20%, Iron 49%, Nutrition Grade A, Based on a 2000 calorie diet

NUTRITIONAL ANALYSIS / GOOD POINTS

Low in saturated fat, No cholesterol, Low in sugar, High in dietary fiber,
High in magnesium, Very high in phosphorus

5 BEAN LEMON AND GARLIC DRESSING SALAD

Beans are a great source of protein, and you will need it during the backyard games of your summer party. Beans are also very versatile and flavorful, especially considering there are many to choose from. This side dish is the best example for there are 5 included! This hearty course will be a perfect complement for a cookout.

Prep Time: 15 Minutes
Cook Time: 25 Minutes
Servings: 6

INGREDIENTS

1/4 c. olive oil
1/4 c. fresh lemon juice
Zest of 1 lemon
1 shallot finely chopped
1 garlic clove, finely minced
1 tbsp. chopped fresh thyme
Kosher salt
Freshly ground black pepper

1 1/2 c. fresh lima beans
1 c. fresh black-eyed peas
1/2 lb. smoked ham hock
1 c. fresh lady peas
1/2 lb. yellow wax beans
1/2 lb. sugar snap peas
1/2 c. chopped almonds
1/4 c. chopped cilantro

DIRECTIONS

⟩ In a mixing container, add oil, lemon juice, garlic, shallot, and thyme. Add salt and pepper to season after it has been whisked.

⟩ In your medium electric skillet, cover and simmer lima beans, black-eyed peas, and ham hock in water for 15-18 minutes. Add lady peas and continue to cook at the same heat for 8-10 minutes. Before draining, take out the ham hock and then cool by running the beans under cold water.

⟩ Bring salted water to a boil in a medium sized electric skillet and cook wax beans and sugar snaps for just a few minutes. Drain all the water out, then to cool run these under cool water as well.

⟩ Add everything together and apply the dressing and toss until all ingredients are coated very nicely!

⟩ This is a hearty mouth-watering meal to smile over! ;)

NUTRITIONAL FACTS:

Serving Size 255 g, Amount Per Serving, Calories 338, Calories from Fat 168, Total Fat 18.7g, Saturated Fat 3.7g, Trans Fat 0.0g, Cholesterol 36mg, Sodium 194mg, Potassium 630mg, Total Carbohydrates 24.5g, Dietary Fiber 7.5g, Sugars 4.8g, Protein 20.3g

Vitamin A 18%, Vitamin C 84%, Calcium 9%, Iron 25%, Nutrition Grade A, Based on a 2000 calorie diet

NUTRITIONAL ANALYSIS / GOOD POINTS
High in thiamin, Very high in vitamin C

JOLLY GREEN BEANS AND SHALLOTS WITH SIZZLING BACON

Even a specific giant would appreciate this flavorful side dish, especially considering bacon is added. However, the meat is not the reason this course is so delightful; you must give the shallots and blue cheese credit as well. This could be a definite addition to the Thanksgiving menu, but also accepted year round!

PREP TIME: 25 MINUTES
Cook Time: 15 Minutes
Servings: 4

INGREDIENTS

1 lb. fresh green beans, trimmed
4 slices bacon
2 shallots, sliced
4 cloves minced garlic
¼ teaspoon salt

¼ teaspoon freshly ground black pepper
1/8 teaspoon ground red pepper (cayenne)
1/3 cup crumbled blue cheese

DIRECTIONS

⟩ Bring 2 quarts of water to a boil in an electric skillet. Cook the green beans for 5 minutes, covered. Fill a pot of ice water, take the beans off the heat and the immediately place them in the water. When they are finally cold then you can drain them.

⟩ While the beans are cooling, cook the bacon until crisp in the skillet; place the bacon on something that will absorb the grease to drain then crumble the bacon after it's dry. Make sure you keep just a little bit of the bacon grease in skillet. (for flavor, of course)

⟩ Using the bacon drippings, cook the shallots over medium heat, turning and mixing while cooking. Mix in the green beans, and season with black and red pepper and salt and cook for just a few minutes while occasionally stirring. (Just enough to heat up the dish)

⟩ Top the bean mixture with cheese and bacon crumbles before serving this delicious delight...Yum! ;)

NUTRITIONAL FACTS:

Serving Size 171 g, Amount Per Serving, Calories 243, Calories from Fat 137, Total Fat 15.2gm, Saturated Fat 6.0gm, Trans Fat 0.0gm, Cholesterol 40mgm, Sodium 968mgm, Potassium 488mgm, Total Carbohydrates 12.2gm, Dietary Fiber 4.0g, Sugars 1.7g, Protein 15.5g

Vitamin A 21%, Vitamin C 34%, Calcium 12%, Iron 10%, Nutrition Grade B+, Based on a 2000 calorie diet

NUTRITIONAL ANALYSIS / GOOD POINTS

Low in sugar
High in phosphorus, High in selenium
High in vitamin C,

MOUNTAINOUS BUTTERMILK MASHED POTATOES

Every cook, beginner or experienced, needs at least one mashed potato recipe, so you might as well go all out with it! Butter, milk, buttermilk for good measure, and of course Yukon gold potatoes make this heavy side dish a force to be reckon with, but too tempting to resist. It would be wise to serve in moderation so there are leftovers for yourself.

Prep Time: 15 Minutes
Cook Time: 35 Minutes
Servings: 8

INGREDIENTS

3/4 cup butter
4 pounds Yukon gold potatoes, peeled and cut into 2-inch pieces
1 tablespoon salt, divided
3/4 cup buttermilk

1/2 cup milk
1/4 teaspoon pepper
Garnishes: fresh parsley, rosemary, and thyme sprigs
1/4 cup chives

DIRECTIONS

> Melt butter in a large electric skillet to melt the butter, frequently stirring over medium heat. Put all but 1-2 tbsp. into a small container and reserve the remainder.

> In a large pot, cover and boil potatoes, water and a few pinches of salt for 15-18 minutes. Drain and then return potatoes to the pot, and cook and a reduced heat for 3-5 minutes, make sure to mix the potatoes while cooking. At this point the potatoes should be dry.

> Using a potato masher, soften the potatoes as desired. (If you do not have a potato masher just use something that will mash up the potatoes) Mix all together the rest of the butter from the bowl, buttermilk, milk, pepper, chives, and the rest of the salt.

> Trickle the reserved butter over the potatoes after transferring them to a serving dish.

> Use more butter for a buttery flavor if desired!

NUTRITIONAL FACTS:

Serving Size 301 g, Amount Per Serving, Calories 361, Calories from Fat 170, Total Fat 18.9g, Saturated Fat 11.7, Cholesterol 48mg, Sodium 1054mg, Potassium 1086mg, Total Carbohydrates 46.6g, Dietary Fiber 6.1g, Sugars 3.4g, Protein 6.7g

Vitamin A 23%, Vitamin C 85%, Calcium 20%, Iron 41%, Nutrition Grade B, Based on a 2000 calorie diet

NUTRITIONAL ANALYSIS / GOOD POINTS
High in iron, Very high in vitamin C

ELECTRIC SKILLET-FRIED OKRA WITH CHICKEN BOUILLON

This side is a charming Southern-style stir-fry. The beauty of the dish is that it is electric skillet-fried instead of deep-fried, leaving it healthier without sacrificing flavor! The tomatoes and lime add freshness to the okra that bodes well with the summer air. A light and tasty side dish for any barbeque.

Prep Time: 15 Minutes
Cook Time: 6 Minutes
Servings: 4

INGREDIENTS

2 pounds' fresh okra
1/2 cup vegetable oil
1 medium-size red onion, thinly sliced
4 cloves minced garlic
2 large tomatoes, seeded and thinly sliced

2 tablespoons lime juice
1 1/2 teaspoons salt
1 1/2 teaspoons pepper
1 teaspoon chicken bouillon granules

DIRECTIONS

> Slice lengthwise to halve the okra.
> Cook okra for 6 minutes in 1/4 cup oil into a large skillet over medium-high. Turn each of the okra frequently and cook in clusters if needed. Drain the vegetable in a colander (paper towels usually work best) until dry and let cool.
> In a large mixing container, combine the remaining ingredients; Toss in the okra and coat. Serve.

NUTRITIONAL FACTS:

Serving Size 359 g, Amount Per Serving, Calories 356, Calories from Fat 252, Total Fat 28.0g, Saturated Fat 5.5g, Cholesterol 0mg, Sodium 902mg, Potassium 926mg, Total Carbohydrates 22.1g, Dietary Fiber 8.7g, Sugars 6.0g, Protein 5.5g

Vitamin A 48%, Vitamin C 115%, Calcium 21%, Iron 11%, Nutrition Grade A-, Based on a 2000 calorie diet

NUTRITIONAL ANALYSIS / GOOD POINTS

No cholesterol, High in manganese, High in vitamin A, Very high in vitamin C

SWEET ORANGE & GINGER BRUSSEL SPROUTS

Brussels sprouts: ick! That is always the consensus, but the dish is misunderstood. How could they be gross with orange and ginger glazed over them? They can't be! This flavorful side will give your diners a different opinion about Brussels sprouts and keep them wanting more.

Prep Time: 10 Minutes
Cook Time: 5 Minutes
Servings: 2

INGREDIENTS

10 to 12 Brussels sprouts
1 tablespoon butter
1 teaspoon grated orange rind
1/4 cup freshly squeezed orange juice

1/4 teaspoon ground ginger
2 tablespoons chopped fresh parsley
1/2 teaspoon cornstarch
1 tablespoon thyme

DIRECTIONS

- Wash and trim Brussels sprouts.
- Have the sprouts and then steam them for 5 minutes. Drain and set aside. (You can boil if desired)
- Add the Brussels sprouts and ground ginger to melted butter in a skillet then season with thyme, salt, and pepper.
- Put in orange juice and add the cornstarch and cook for about 3 minutes, mixing them until the sauce begins to become richen and thick.
- Garnish with parsley after transferring to a dish where you will serve them.
- Delicious!! ;)

NUTRITIONAL FACTS:

Serving Size 140 g, Amount Per Serving, Calories 115, Calories from Fat 57, Total Fat 6.3g, Saturated Fat 3.8g, Cholesterol 15mg, Sodium 68mg, Potassium 470mg, Total Carbohydrates 14.0g, Dietary Fiber 4.4g, Sugars 4.7g, Protein 3.8g

Vitamin A 25%, Vitamin C 189%, Calcium 7%, Iron 19%, Nutrition Grade A, Based on a 2000 calorie diet

NUTRITIONAL ANALYSIS / GOOD POINTS

High in dietary fiber, High in iron, High in manganese, High in potassium, Very high in vitamin A, Very high in vitamin B6, Very high in vitamin C

CREAMY PEARLED ONION SPINACH
WITH AND BACON

Pearl onions are an elegant addition to most meals, and a way to contain the flavor of one of the most used vegetables. They complement well with spinach and cream, and bacon once again offers its unique essence to the course. The best of all worlds are mixed together in this side!

Prep Time: 10 Minutes
Cook Time: 30 Minutes
Servings: 4

INGREDIENTS

1 1/4 pounds' spinach
10 ounces' white pearl onions (about 2 1/2 cups)
6 cloves minced garlic
5 tablespoons unsalted butter
2 tablespoons all-purpose flour
1 1/4 cups milk

3 ounces' slab bacon, cut into 1/4-inch dice (about 3/4 cups)
Coarse salt and freshly ground pepper
Generous pinch of freshly grated nutmeg
1/2 cup heavy cream
2 teaspoons lemon juice

DIRECTIONS

- Cook washed spinach, covered in a large pot over medium heat, for 1 minute. Stir, recover, and cook for an additional minute. Remove the cover and stir until leaves are wilted or turning cooked.
- Rinse spinach under cold water using a colander. Pat dry with paper towel (kitchen towel works as well) then chop to make the spinach finely cut up.
- Boil onions and garlic in water for 3-4 minutes in an electric skillet. Save the water in the pot after removing onions and garlic; rinse them with cold water and trim the onions after rinsing them.
- Place the onions back into water that was cooking and cook for 10-12 minutes. After draining, rinse in cold water again.
- Whisk together flour and melted butter in an electric skillet over medium heat until smooth. While whisking, slowly add milk and boil for one minute then remove from the heat.
- Using a different electric skillet, melt the rest of the butter on low to medium heat. Cook bacon for 6 minutes then add onions and spinach. Put in the mixture with the milk and the cream. Continue to cook, adding 1/4 teaspoon pepper, 1 teaspoon salt, and nutmeg while continuing to stir frequently for 10 more minutes, but avoid bringing to a boil. Add the lemon juice and a pinch of salt and pepper to your liking.

NUTRITIONAL FACTS:

Serving Size 356 g, Amount Per Serving, Calories 416, Calories from Fat 280, Total Fat 31.1g, Saturated Fat 16.6g, Trans Fat 0.0g, Cholesterol 88mg, Sodium 1333mg, Potassium 1106mg, Total Carbohydrates 21.1g, Dietary Fiber 5.0g, Sugars 7.2g, Protein 16.4g

Vitamin A 280%, Vitamin C 79%. Calcium 28%, Iron 26%, Nutrition Grade B+, Based on a 2000 calorie diet

NUTRITIONAL ANALYSIS / GOOD POINTS

High in manganese, Very high in vitamin A, High in vitamin B6, High in vitamin C

BUTTERY POTATOES TOSSED WITH PARSLEY

Sometimes appearance can go a long way, and when it comes to cooking, it is worth it, and it's simple! These boiled potatoes are a delicious hearty meal, but chopped parsley mixed in provides a great sight and a great taste with little work involved.

Prep Time: 10 Minutes
Cook Time: 20 Minutes
Servings: 4

INGREDIENTS

2 pounds small red potatoes
2 teaspoons coarse salt
2 tablespoons unsalted butter

2 tablespoons roughly chopped fresh
flat-leaf parsley
1/4 cup chopped green onions
Freshly ground pepper

DIRECTIONS

> For each potato, peel the middle.
> Cover the potatoes with cold water in a large electric skillet and bring to a boil. Reduce the heat to medium and cook for 20 minutes or until potatoes are soft in the center.
> Use a colander to drain them, then put them back into the electric skillet while it's still warm. Add the butter, green onions, and parsley and toss it all together, then season with ground pepper. Serve while still warm.

NUTRITIONAL FACTS:

Serving Size 252 g, Amount Per Serving, Calories 230, Calories from Fat 57, Total Fat 6.3g, Saturated Fat 3.8g, Cholesterol 15mg, Sodium 1020mg, Potassium 1151mg, Total Carbohydrates 41.2g, Dietary Fiber 6.0g, Sugars 2.5g, Protein 5.3g

Vitamin A 9%, Vitamin C 41%, Calcium 6%, Iron 22%, Nutrition Grade A-, Based on a 2000 calorie diet

NUTRITIONAL ANALYSIS / GOOD POINTS

Low in cholesterol, High in dietary fiber, High in manganese, High in potassium, High in vitamin C

REFRESHING VEGGIE & HERB RATATOUILLE

There is no need for the assistance of a cartoon rat to cook this easy side dish, you just need plenty of vegetables and you're set! The zucchini and eggplant give the meal plenty of substance and the spices and flavorings bring it all together. Mix everything into a sauté electric skillet and enjoy!

Prep Time: 30 Minutes
Cook Time: 30 Minutes
Servings: 4

INGREDIENTS

1 Tbsp. olive oil
1 medium sized red onion, peeled and diced
3 cloves of garlic, chopped
1 red bell pepper, seeded and diced
1 medium Italian eggplant, diced
2 tomatoes, seeded and diced

1 zucchini, trimmed and diced
salt and freshly ground pepper
juice of 1/2 a lemon
2 Tbsp. fresh basil, chopped
2 Tbsp. chopped Oregano
extra-virgin olive oil to taste
several leaves of basil, chiffonade

DIRECTIONS

> Add olive oil in a large electric skillet over medium-high heat.
> Sauté and mix onions for 2 minutes in oil, adding the garlic after and cooking for an additional minute.
> Sauté the red pepper and eggplant for 3-5 minutes, being mindful of the heat because you do not want the vegetables to burn.
> Cook the tomato and zucchini and season with salt (just for a little flavor.) Add pepper and squeeze in lemon juice. The zucchini should be ready when it's tender.
> After mixing in the oregano and basil quickly take it off the heat.
> Garnish with basil and sprinkle a light amount of olive oil over the dish.

NUTRITIONAL FACTS:

Serving Size 281 g, Amount Per Serving, Calories 105, Calories from Fat 40, Total Fat 4.5g, Saturated Fat 0.7g, Cholesterol 0mg, Sodium 595mg, Potassium 678mg, Total Carbohydrates 16.2g, Dietary Fiber 7.4g, Sugars 7.8g, Protein 3.2g

Vitamin A 36%, Vitamin C 103%, Calcium 7%, Iron 11%, Nutrition Grade A, Based on a 2000 calorie diet

NUTRITIONAL ANALYSIS / GOOD POINTS

No cholesterol, Very high in dietary fiber, High in iron, Very high in manganese, High in magnesium, High in potassium, Very high in vitamin A, High in vitamin B6, Very high in vitamin C

SWEET & SIMPLE GARLIC SEARED ASPARAGUS

There won't be an easier dish to make that provides this much flavor from basic ingredients. Asparagus goes well with most main courses, so having the vegetable as a side is always a smart decision. Garlic, asparagus, salt and pepper, and enjoy! It's that simple.

Prep Time: 5 Minutes
Cook Time: 15 Minutes
Servings: 4

INGREDIENTS

1 pound fresh asparagus spears, trimmed
3 cloves garlic, minced
1/4 teaspoon ground black pepper
1 teaspoon coarse salt

1 teaspoon red pepper flakes
1 teaspoon cayenne
2 tablespoons olive oil
1/4 cup butter

DIRECTIONS

> Season asparagus with red pepper and cayenne.
> In a skillet over medium high heat add butter. Once melted, mix in olive oil and salt and pepper. First cook the garlic for a minute, adding the asparagus afterwards and continuing to cook for an additional 8-10 minutes, turning occasionally to verify they have cooked evenly.
> Delicious and simple…tasty meal packed with vitamins! Delicious! ;)

NUTRITION FACTS

Serving Size 140 g, Amount Per Serving, Calories 191, Calories from Fat 169, Total Fat 18.8g, Saturated Fat 8.4g. Cholesterol 31mg. Sodium 565mg. Potassium 261mg. Total Carbohydrates 5.7g, Dietary Fiber 2.7g, Sugars 2.3g, Protein 2.9g

Vitamin A 32%, Vitamin C 13%, Calcium 4%, Iron 14%, Nutrition Grade C+, Based on a 2000 calorie diet

NUTRITIONAL ANALYSIS / GOOD POINTS

High in vitamin A

VEGGIE BOATS FOR MEAT SAILORS

Your parents told you never to play with your food, but then offered you "Ants on a Log." This is the adult version; instead of celery you have zucchini, and instead of raisins and peanut butter you have beef and cheese! Go ahead and play with your food, you've earned it.

Prep Time: 10 Minutes
Cook Time: 10 Minutes
Servings: 4

INGREDIENTS

4 medium zucchini, halved and scooped
1 tablespoon olive oil
1/2 white onion, diced
2 cloves minced garlic
1 jalapeño pepper, seeded and diced

1 pound ground beef
1 teaspoon ground cumin
1/2 cup salsa
1 cup grated cheddar cheese
Salt and pepper
Fresh cilantro, to garnish

DIRECTIONS

> Cut the zucchini and scoop out seeds. Make sure to halve long ways.
> Add olive oil to a skillet over medium-high heat. Cook the onions, garlic, and peppers for 3-4 minutes, just enough to soften in the electric skillet. Sprinkle a few pinches of salt and pepper each to season.
> Next, season the ground beef with cumin and place in the electric skillet. You will cook this in with the vegetables. After the beef, has browned, put in salsa and stir until everything is combined.
> Mix in the cheddar cheese after removing the skillet from the heat.
> Make sure each zucchini receives the same amount of beef filling and then grill the boats for 5 or 6 minutes. Make sure that the zucchini does not get to be too soft and fragile.
> You may use cilantro to garnish and dust cheese over the top. Make sure it's warm when served.

NUTRITIONAL FACTS:

Serving Size 406 g, Amount Per Serving, Calories 410, Calories from Fat 185, Total Fat 20.6g, Saturated Fat 9.2g, Cholesterol 131mg, Sodium 1051mg, Potassium 1189mg, Total Carbohydrates 12.0g, Dietary Fiber 3.6g1, Sugars 5.5g, Protein 45.0g

Vitamin A 26%, Vitamin C 68%, Calcium 26%, Iron 128%, Nutrition Grade A-, Based on a 2000 calorie diet

NUTRITIONAL ANALYSIS / GOOD POINTS

Very high in iron, High in phosphorus, High in selenium, Very high in vitamin B6, Very high in vitamin B12, High in vitamin C, High in zinc

FRESH AND VIGOROUS VEGGIE PASTA

For all the vegetarians, out there, this pasta is a perfect dish, and don't worry, carnivores, it's okay to take a break from the meat occasionally, you're allowed to! Fresh zucchini and peppers sautéed and served with mozzarella over pasta seems simple enough and it is. The dish is light, but enough will leave you full and satisfied no matter your food preference.

Prep Time: 10 Minutes
Cook Time: 20 Minutes
Servings: 4

INGREDIENTS

2 tbsp. unsalted butter
1 tbsp. extra-virgin olive oil
3 small bell peppers, orange, yellow, and red, thinly sliced
1 small onion, thinly sliced
4 cloves garlic, minced
Kosher salt
Freshly ground black pepper

2 medium zucchini, cut into 1/2"-thick slices
12 oz. fettuccine pasta
4 oz. smoked mozzarella, grated (about 1 cup) + more for serving
1/8 c. fresh basil, torn
1/8 c. fresh oregano, torn

DIRECTIONS

> Using the package directions, cook pasta. Keep at least a cup of the water from the pasta and drain the rest from the pasta.
> Meanwhile...combine butter and oil, peppers, garlic, and onion, along with salt and pepper seasoning in your skillet and cook over medium heat. Make sure you cook for at least 10 minutes, stirring occasionally. Lastly, cook the zucchini for 4-6 minutes, stirring in the flavor.
> Season the pepper mixture with basil, oregano, salt and pepper, then add the pasta, mozzarella, and ½ cup of the reserved pasta water. Keep tossing the mixture until it is all coated with the sauce mixture.
> Sprinkle the dish with more mozzarella, fresh basil and oregano if desired.

NUTRITIONAL FACTS:

Serving Size 301 g, Amount Per Serving, Calories 492, Calories from Fat 191, Total Fat 21.2g, Saturated Fat 10.5g, Cholesterol 107mg, Sodium 291mg, Potassium 633mg, Total Carbohydrates 57.6g, Dietary Fiber 3.7g, Sugars 5.0g, Protein 19.1g

Vitamin A 53%, Vitamin C 152%, Calcium 28%, Iron 26%, Nutrition Grade B, Based on a 2000 calorie diet

NUTRITIONAL ANALYSIS / GOOD POINTS
High in vitamin A, Very high in vitamin C

CHAPTER 15:
SWEETS AND DESSERTS:

I can never say enough about this section and I won't stop now! These recipes will have you playing like a kid in the candy store. These "kiss cuddling" desserts will add a special romance to that sweet tooth you already have. This section is the best way to make up with anyone, even yourself. So, snuggle up a date with one of the dazzling dessert selections. You will easily fall in love...but don't worry...they will never break your heart!

NO-SUGAR HONEY APPLE FLIPPED UPSIDE DOWN CAKE

This no-sugar apple upside down cake will satisfy your sweet tooth. The honey and molasses in the cake is often used as a substitute and is just as sweet as sugar, if not more. This is a dessert that you will want to keep making over and over again.

Prep Time: 20 Minutes
Cook Time: 20 Minutes
Servings: 8

INGREDIENTS

1 ¾ cups all-purpose flour
1 ½ tsp. sea salt
1 tsp. ground cinnamon
¾ tsp. baking soda
½ tsp. baking powder
¾ cup mild-flavored (light) molasses
¼ cup honey

1 large egg
2 tsps. grated peeled ginger
1/3 cup the cream
¼ cup whole milk
3-4 peeled honey crisp or pink lady apples

DIRECTIONS -

> Prepare and stir flour, salt, cinnamon, baking soda and baking powder in a mixing bowl.
> In another bowl combine honey, molasses, egg, ginger, the cream and milk and mix thoroughly and set bowl to the side. (Keep a little bit of sugar and butter to caramelize apples)
> Cut apples and separate the cores.
> Add apples to a non-stick skillet and cook for 3 minutes on each side along with some of the sugar and butter that you left over.
> Put the cake batter over the top and bake for 35 minutes at 325 degrees. (Check cake with tooth pick to see if it is cooked through)
> Cool for at least 15 min and serve.
> (Served best with Vanilla Ice Cream)

NUTRITIONAL FACTS:

Calories (kcal) 360 , Fat (g) 10 , Saturated Fat (g) 6 , Cholesterol (mg) 55 , Carbohydrates (g) 68 , Dietary Fiber (g) 3, Total Sugars (g) 39, Protein (g) 4, Sodium (mg) 540

THE ALL-AMERICAN HONEY APPLE PIE IN A SKILLET

This isn't Grandma's apple pie but believe me she wouldn't know the difference. This All-American Apple Pie uses a refrigerated crust topped with apples, cinnamon and brown sugar. It's a dessert that will leave the whole family begging for second servings.

Prep Time: 20 Minutes
Cook Time: 1 hour 10 Minutes
Servings: 8

INGREDIENTS

2 cups Granny Smith apples
2 lbs. Braeburn apples
1 tsp. ground cinnamon
¾ cup granulated sugar
½ cup butter

1 cup brown sugar
¼ cup honey
7 oz. pie crusts (refrigerated package)
1 egg white
(Butter pecan ice cream if desired)

DIRECTIONS

> Prepare apples: peel and cut. Cover in cinnamon and sugar.
> In a non-stick skillet add brown sugar and butter. Cook until sugar is liquefied for 1 to 1 ½ minutes.
> Turn off heat and put piecrust down over the brown sugar in the electric skillet.
> Add the apples to the piecrust and cover with the remaining piecrust.
> Add a coat of the egg whites and sugar to the top of the piecrust. (use a brush)
> Create several slits on the top for best baking results.
> Bake at 345º for about 1 hour and 15 minutes.
> Cool for at least 30 min on a towel or rack
> Best served with Vanilla ice cream.

NUTRITIONAL FACTS:

Serving Size 232 g, Amount Per Serving, Calories 480, Calories from Fat 183, Total Fat 20.4g, Saturated Fat 9.4g, Trans Fat 0.0g, Cholesterol 31mg, Sodium 227mg, Potassium 208mg, Total Carbohydrates 76.7g, Dietary Fiber 4.0g, Sugars 59.8g, Protein 2.6g

Vitamin A 7%, Vitamin C 18%, Calcium 3%, Iron 9%, Nutrition Grade C, Based on a 2000 calorie diet

NUTRITIONAL ANALYSIS / GOOD POINTS
Low in cholesterol, Low in sodium, Very high in vitamin B6

MILK DIPPING CHOCOLATE CHIP COOKIE

You will love this recipe. No longer will you need a mixer or a cookie sheet to make cookies. You can make them all, right here, in the non-stick electric skillet.

Prep Time: 20 Minutes
Cook Time: 40 Minutes
Servings: 4

INGREDIENTS

3 cups all-purpose flour
1 ¼ tsp. baking soda
1 ½ tsp. salt
¾ cup butter, melted and cooled slightly
1 ¼ cups brown sugar

1 cup sugar
3 eggs
2 tsp. vanilla extract
1 teaspoon cinnamon
2 ½ cups chocolate chips

DIRECTIONS

> Prepare: combine the flour, baking soda and salt in a mixing container.
> In a separate mixing container, combine butter, cinnamon and brown sugar, then add the eggs and the vanilla extract.
> Add the chocolate chips and the dry ingredients and mix together.
> Flatten the dough in a non-stick skillet and bake for 25 minutes at 325 degrees. When it starts to brown on the edges let it cook for about 5 more minutes
> Cookies must cool for about 15-20 min before serving...Yummy!

NUTRITIONAL FACTS:

Serving Size 376 g, Amount Per Serving, Calories 1,623, Calories from Fat 629, Total Fat 69.9g, Saturated Fat 44.8g, Trans Fat 0.0g, Cholesterol 238mg, Sodium 1655mg, Potassium 611mg, Total Carbohydrates 229.4g, Dietary Fiber 6.4g, Sugars 148.9g, Protein 22.3g

Vitamin A 28%, Vitamin C 0%, Calcium 28%, Iron 43%, Nutrition Grade D-

SUMMER SWEET BERRY ECSTACY DELIGHT

For those fruit lovers, out there, there is nothing better than a nice warm berry cobbler. The Skillet Berry Delight is a cobbler in disguise and produces just the right number of berries with a warm flaky crust.

Prep Time: 10 Minutes
Cook Time: 10 Minutes
Servings: 8

INGREDIENTS

2 lbs. fresh mixed berries
¼ cup plus 2 tbsps. Sugar
1 tbsps. Water
1 tbsp. fresh lemon juice
1 cup all-purpose flour
1 tsp. baking powder

½ tsp. baking soda
pinch of salt
½ cup plus 2 tbsps. Low-fat buttermilk
2 tbsps. Melted unsalted butter
1/8 tsp. ground cinnamon mixed with
1 tsp. sugar

DIRECTIONS

> Prepare: In a mixing bowl combine the flour, baking powder. Baking soda, salt, 2 tablespoons sugar, buttermilk and butter. Create a dough.
> In a non-stick skillet add the berries with the water, lemon juice and ¼ cup of sugar.
> Cook for 15 minutes. Mix will thicken the longer you cook it.
> Spoon the dough over the fruit and season with cinnamon-sugar.
> Cover with aluminum foil and cook for 20 minutes.
> Let it cool about 15-20 min...then Serve

NUTRITIONAL FACTS

Serving Size 159 g, Amount Per Serving, Calories 178, Calories from Fat 32, Total Fat 3.6g, Saturated Fat 1.9g, Trans Fat 0.0g, Cholesterol 8mg, Sodium 137mg, Potassium 253mg, Total Carbohydrates 33.0g, Dietary Fiber 4.5g, Sugars 15.2g, Protein 3.0g

Vitamin A 2%, Vitamin C 42%, Calcium 7%, Iron 8%, Nutrition Grade B, Based on a 2000 calorie diet

NUTRITIONAL ANALYSIS / GOOD POINTS

Low in cholesterol, Very high in vitamin C

SWEET TART BROWN SUGAR PEAR PIE

This tart pear pie is a perfect recipe for a perfect day. The tartness of the pie, paired with cinnamon and the doughtiness of the crust can bring anyone back to the days of their childhood.

Prep Time: 10 Minutes
Cook Time: 40 Minutes
Servings: 4

INGREDIENTS

15 oz. pie crust (2 9-inch unbaked pastry pie crusts)
¾ tsp. ground ginger
1 tsp. ground cinnamon
½ tsp. salt
1/3 cup granulated sugar
1/3 cup firmly packed brown sugar

2 tbsp. freshly squeezed lemon juice
1 cup heavy cream
7 fresh Bartlett pears, peeled and sliced
1 large egg yolk
3 tbsp. heavy cream
1 tsp. light brown sugar

DIRECTIONS -

> Prepare: in a mixing container, combine sliced pears, flour, ginger, cinnamon, lemon juice, cream and sugars.
> Mix butter, ¾ cup sugar for 3 minutes. Add the flour mixture and buttermilk.
> Put the pear mixture directly into pie crust.
> in a non-stick electric skillet add the batter over the pie crust.
> Bake at 350 for 30 minutes.
> Cool and serve with ice cream and caramel sauce if desired.
> Serve with ice cream for this delicious treat! (optional)

NUTRITIONAL FACTS:

Serving Size 556 g, Amount Per Serving, Calories 1,043, Calories from Fat 484, Total Fat 53.8g, Saturated Fat 19.1g, Trans Fat 0.0g Cholesterol 109mg, Sodium 894mg, Potassium 565mg, Total Carbohydrates 137.6g, Dietary Fiber 13.5g, Sugars 65.2g, Protein 9.8g

Vitamin A 15%, Vitamin C 33%, Calcium 9%, Iron 23%, Nutrition Grade C, Based on a 2000 calorie diet

I LOVE BUTTERMILK FRUIT PLUM CAKE SKILLET–

This is such a versatile dessert that you change it up according to season. This is a great way to ensure that your cake will never get old and that it will also be a hit at every party. Switch it up with different fruits every time you make it...It's delicious and FUN!!!

Prep Time: 10 Minutes
Cook Time: 45 Minutes
Servings: 4

INGREDIENTS

4 tbsp. unsalted butter
1 cup all-purpose flour
½ tsp. baking powder
¼ tsp. baking soda
½ tsp. salt

¾ cup sugar (plus 2 tbsp.)
1 large egg
½ cup buttermilk
2 ripe sliced medium plums

DIRECTIONS

> With an electric mixture combine butter, ¾ sugar, egg, flour and buttermilk for 5 minutes.
> In a non-stick electric skillet add the batter and arrange the plums overlapping them in rows on top with the rest of the sugar.
> Bake at 325 at 30 minutes.
> Cool and serve.

NUTRITIONAL FACTS

Serving Size 219 g, Amount Per Serving, Calories 434, Calories from Fat 122, Total Fat 13.5g, Saturated Fat 7.9g , Trans Fat 0.0g, Cholesterol 78mg, Sodium 504mg, Potassium 261mg, Total Carbohydrates 75.8g, Dietary Fiber 3.1g, Sugars 48.6g, Protein 6.2g
Vitamin A 8%, Vitamin C 12%, Calcium 8%, Iron 12%, Nutrition Grade C+, Based on a 2000 calorie diet

WARM BACKYARD S'MORE BROWNIES

S'Mores have always been an indispensable dessert of the outdoors either camping or just enjoying a nice evening at home. With these blondies, you can skip the fire pit and have delicious S'Mores ready to eat whenever everyone is ready! Then bring them back outside for the full experience without the mess.

Prep Time: 30 Minutes
Cook Time: 2 Hours
Servings: 24

INGREDIENTS

8 tablespoons (1 stick) unsalted butter, plus more for the electric skillet
1 cup all-purpose flour, spooned and leveled
2 teaspoons baking powder
1 teaspoon kosher salt
1 ½ cups packed light brown sugar

2 teaspoons pure vanilla extract
2 large eggs
1 cup pecans, coarsely chopped
4 graham crackers, broken into small pieces
1 cup miniature marshmallows
1/2 cup semisweet chocolate chips
1/4 cup white chocolate chips

DIRECTIONS

> Line The electric skillet with buttered aluminum foil. Mix the flour, baking powder, and salt together in a bowl.
> Melt the butter in an electric skillet over medium heat. Take away from heat to add the brown sugar and vanilla. Beat in and combine eggs, then combine the flour mixture; lastly, add pecans.
> Evenly put the mixture into the prepared electric skillet and bake for 20-25 minutes. Cover the top with the graham crackers, marshmallows, and chocolate and white chocolate chips and continue to cook for 7-8 more minutes. Make sure the electric skillet cools entirely on a wire rack. Use the foil to easily help take out the blondies. Divide into 24 bars.

NUTRITIONAL FACTS:

Serving Size 41 g, Amount Per Serving, Calories 178, Calories from Fat 85, Total Fat 9.4g, Saturated Fat 4.2g, Trans Fat 0.0g, Cholesterol 26mg, Sodium 189mg, Potassium 110mg, Total Carbohydrates 22.1g, Dietary Fiber 1.0g, Sugars 14.2g, Protein 2.4g

Vitamin A 3%, Vitamin C 0%, Calcium 4%, Iron 4%, Nutrition Grade D-, Based on a 2000 calorie diet

BULLWINKLE'S RICH AND SMOOTH, WHIPPED CHOCOLATE TEMPTATION

Of course, we're not talking about a moose, cartoon or real, but mousse: the creamy and fluffy chocolate delight. With strong coffee or espresso hints, depending on what you prefer, this tempting dessert is one of the best recipes, and very essential to the sweet tooth's repertoire!

If you want to turn heads…Make This Dessert! "It's Amazing!" ;)

Prep Time: 1 Day (Optional)
Cook Time: 2 Hours 10 Minutes (2 Hours Chilled)
Servings: 6

INGREDIENTS

¾ Cup Chilled Heavy Cream, Divided
4 Large egg yolks
1/4 cup espresso, room temperature
1/4 tsp. vanilla extract
3 tbsp. sugar, divided

1/8 tsp. kosher salt
6 oz. semisweet chocolate (60-72% cacao), chopped
2 Large egg whites

DIRECTIONS

- Whisk ½ cup cream and fluff until it forms firm tips; then cover the cream for it to chill.
- In a metal mixing container, mix together egg yolks, espresso, vanilla extract, salt, and 2 tbsp. sugar. Carefully place the bowl over barely simmering water, but make sure it does not encounter the water. Cook and continue to stir for 1 minute or until mixture has appeared to double in size and lighten in color. (you will tell that it will start to grow)
- Take the bowl away from the electric skillet and put in chocolate; mix until blended. Put aside until it reaches room temperature while seldom stirring so it sets correctly.
- With the assistance of an electric mixer, beat egg white in a different bowl. Slowly add remaining sugar. Turn up speed and mix until it starts to form firm tips with the mixture.
- Fold egg whites and chocolate twice through and do the same with the whipped cream and mixture and make sure it is blended.
- Evenly split mousse and chill for 2 hours at the least. It must have time to get firm.
- Stir ¼ cup cream in a small bowl until firm tips form; spoon over mousse, serve.

Electric Skillet Cookbook Complete

Serving Size 82 g, Amount Per Serving, Calories 252, Calories from Fat 154, Total Fat 17.1g, Saturated Fat 9.6g, Trans Fat 0.0g, Cholesterol 160mg, Sodium 77mg, Potassium 157mg, Total Carbohydrates 24.8g, Dietary Fiber 1.7g, Sugars 21.6g, Protein 4.5g

Vitamin A 8%, Vitamin C 0%, Calcium 3%, Iron 7%, Nutrition Grade D, Based on a 2000 calorie diet

NUTRITIONAL ANALYSIS / GOOD POINTS

Low in sodium

HEAVENLY ORANGE VANILLA ANGEL'S FOOD CAKE

Nothing is as sweet and fluffy as Angel's food cake, and nothing offers more variety regarding what you're able to accompany the dessert with. Fruit, cream, chocolate, the possibilities are endless, and it allows the cook to be creative as long as the sweetness isn't overwhelmed by some odd addition; to each their own though!

Prep Time: 20 Minutes
Cook Time: 35 Minutes
Servings: 12

INGREDIENTS

1 3/4 cups sugar
1/4 teaspoon salt
1 cup cake flour, sifted
12 egg whites (the closer to room temperature the better)

1/3 cup warm water
1/2 tsp. orange extract
1/2 tsp. vanilla extract
1 1/2 teaspoons cream of tartar

DIRECTIONS

> Using an electric mixer, stir sugar for 2 minutes. At this point you want to sift together half of the sugar and combine with salt and cake flour. Put aside the extra sugar.
> In another bowl, mix and combine the egg whites, water, orange and vanilla extracts, and cream of tartar and blend well. Let sit for 2 minutes then sift in the extra sugar, continuously whisking. Sift and sprinkle flour mixture on the foam to form tips. Fold until mixture is combined.
> Using an ungreased tube electric skillet, spread the mixture evenly. Bake for 35 minutes.
> On a wire rack, let the cake cool upside down for 1 hour at the least.
> Yummy! ;)

NUTRITIONAL FACTS:

Serving Size 80 g, Amount Per Serving, Calories 167, Calories from Fat 1, Total Fat 0.2g, Cholesterol 0mg, Sodium 84mg, Potassium 128mg, Total Carbohydrates 37.6g, Sugars 29.5g, Protein 4.7g

Vitamin A 0%, Vitamin C 0%, Calcium 0%, Iron 3%, Nutrition Grade D+, Based on a 2000 calorie diet

NUTRITIONAL ANALYSIS / GOOD POINTS

Very low in saturated fat, No cholesterol, Low in sodium

MAGNIFICENT MINI STRAWBERRY MASCARPONE INDULGENCES

Mascarpone is a soft and mild Italian cream cheese and is light and sweet enough to make any dessert incredibly tasteful. When in cupcake form, the flavor is so versatile that any glaze or icing will do, and in this case, strawberry is the weapon of choice. Enjoy this great delicacy!

Prep Time: 20 Minutes
Cook Time: 20 Minutes
Servings: 48

INGREDIENTS

8 ounces' mascarpone cheese (about 1 cup), softened
2 egg whites
1/4 cup vegetable oil
1 box white cake mix

1 cup water
1/3 cup frozen strawberries, thawed and drained
2 1/2 cups powdered sugar
1/4 tsp. vanilla extract

DIRECTIONS

❯ Turn on to 350 degrees F the oven to preheat. Use a mini-muffin baking tin and line each with baking cups.

❯ Mix together the mascarpone cheese, egg whites, and vegetable oil together. Whisk until creamy. Mix in the water and cake mix until even with a nice creamy consistency. Fill each mini cup almost to the top and bake for 18-20 minutes (they will start to turn a golden color.) After removal, let the cupcakes cool while still in the tin for 5 minutes, then place them on a wire rack where they will sit.

❯ In the meantime, while cupcakes are baking, use a blender to puree the strawberries; then mix with the powdered sugar and vanilla extract in a bowl until velvety. Spread the glaze on top of each cupcake after they have completely cooled.

Note: "For the Vanilla Lovers!" Adding a little extra vanilla will give that little extra kiss for your taste buds! ;)

NUTRITIONAL FACTS:

Serving Size 30 g, Amount Per Serving, Calories 90, Calories from Fat 27, Total Fat 2.9g, Saturated Fat 0.8g, Trans Fat 0.0g, Cholesterol 2mg, Sodium 78mg, Potassium 20mg, Total Carbohydrates 15.0g, Sugars 12.1g, Protein 1.2g

Vitamin A 0%, Vitamin C 1%, Calcium 3%, Iron 1%, Nutrition Grade D, Based on a 2000 calorie diet

NUTRITIONAL ANALYSIS / GOOD POINTS
Low in cholesterol

VELVETY NO-BAKE ITALIAN HAZELNUT COCOA COOKIES

The spread most people have come to crave can be made into delicious cookie form. Mixed in with some oats and a hint of vanilla, these no-bake cookies are easy and quick to make, and sure to please the family after a good meal. Enjoy with milk if desired!

Prep Time: 15 Minutes
Cook Time: 15 Minutes
Servings: 14

INGREDIENTS

2 cups sugar
2 tablespoons butter
½ cup milk
1 teaspoon vanilla

1/4 teaspoon powdered sugar
3/4 cup hazelnut cocoa spread
2 cups old-fashioned oats

DIRECTIONS

> Use parchment paper on the skillet.
> Boil 2 cups sugar, 2 tablespoons butter and 1/2 cup milk in a 4-quart electric skillet over medium heat. Take off heat after 1 minute of boiling.
> Combine 1 teaspoon vanilla and 3/4 cup a hazelnut cocoa spread (a few brands out there...Nutella is what I use) until well blended and soft, and then add the oats and stir until even.
> Spoon even glops onto the sheet, each should be about 2 tablespoons per cookie. Sprinkle with powdered sugar after they have completely cooled.

NUTRITIONAL FACTS:

Serving Size 65g, Amount Per Serving, Calories 253, Calories from Fat 86, Total Fat 9.5g, Saturated Fat 2.8g, Cholesterol 5mg, Sodium 80mg, Potassium 138mg, Total Carbohydrates 39.7g, Dietary Fiber 2.0g, Sugars 30.5g, Protein 5.3g

Vitamin A 1%, Vitamin C 0%, Calcium 2%, Iron 10%
Nutrition Grade C-, Based on a 2000 calorie diet

NUTRITIONAL ANALYSIS / GOOD POINTS

Very low in cholesterol, Low in sodium, Very high in vitamin B6

CREAMY NO-OVEN PB&C

Peanut butter and jelly is a meal, but peanut butter and chocolate make a tempting after-hours treat. Despite what many may think, both don't have to be baked and both aren't required to be unhealthy, too unhealthy that is. With the additions of reduced-fat cream cheese and Greek yogurt, this is a dessert worth trying!

Prep Time: 10 Minutes
Cook Time: 4 Hours
Servings: 12

INGREDIENTS

CRUST
Cooking spray
24 chocolate wafer cookies
3 tablespoons unsalted butter, melted
2 ounces' semisweet chocolate morsels, melted
2 oz.' white chocolate morsels, melted

FILLING

4 ounces reduced-fat cream cheese
1/2 cup creamy all-natural peanut butter
1/2 cup 2-percent Greek yogurt
2/3 cup confectioners' sugar

TOPPING
1/4 cup chopped roasted unsalted peanuts
Kosher salt

DIRECTIONS

> **Crust:** Completely line an 8-inch square electric skillet with foil that has been scarcely coated with cooking spray. Grind cookies in a food processor (A blender work as well) until crumbled fine. Melt butter and blend with the crumbs to coat. Next, melt the chocolate and mix in until pasty. Firmly spread the mixture into the bottom of the electric skillet, and place in the refrigerator, covered.

> **Filling and topping:** Clean the food processor for you will need it for making the filling. Mix together the cream cheese, peanut butter, yogurt and sugar in the processor until you see it get smooth in texture. Take the crust out of the refrigerator and spread the blended mix over the crust until it is covered evenly all over. Sprinkle the peanuts across the top and add a pinch of salt. Re-cover and place back in the refrigerator for at least 4 hours, or for even better results, overnight.

> Loosen the mixture around the edges, and then use the foil to carefully lift it out of the electric skillet. Divide into 12 bars.

NUTRITIONAL FACTS:

Serving Size 230 g, Amount Per Serving, Calories 914, Calories from Fat 518, Total Fat 57.6g, Saturated Fat 27.4g, Cholesterol 125mg, Sodium 498mg, Potassium 394mg, Total Carbohydrates 88.6g, Dietary Fiber 3.1g, Sugars 80.0g, Protein 18.0g

Vitamin A 31%, Vitamin C 0%, Calcium 13%, Iron 17%, Nutrition Grade C-, Based on a 2000 calorie diet

SOFT CLASSIC VANILLA CHOCOLATE CHIP COOKIES

Chocolate chip cookies are the most famous cookie, and certainly one of the more well-known desserts so there have been many variations along the way. So, what's better than the best? The best of the best! Simple. Quick. Delightful.

Prep Time: 30 Minutes
Cook Time: 14 Minutes
Servings: 60

INGREDIENTS

3/4 cup butter, softened
3/4 cup granulated sugar
3/4 cup firmly packed dark brown sugar
2 large eggs
1 3/4 teaspoons vanilla extract

2 1/4 cups plus 2 Tbsp. all-purpose flour
1 teaspoon baking soda
3/4 teaspoon salt
1 1/2 (12-oz.) packages semisweet chocolate morsels

DIRECTIONS

> Mix butter and until it becomes creamy then beat in eggs and 1 1/2 tsp. vanilla, until well blended.
> Steadily add to butter mixture (In a separate mixing container) the flour, baking soda, and salt, and mix together until smooth. Add the morsels and stir until they are evenly throughout. Scoop tablespoon-sized balls onto a skillet lined with parchment paper so they don't stick.
> Bake 12-15 minutes or to your liking. Let cool for at least 15 minutes.

Note: you can get creative with the things you can substitute (or combine) in this recipe for chocolate chips! A few of the favorites are: Cranberries, nuts, raisins, blueberries, cherries, caramel chips, white chocolate chips!

If you have an idea for a substitute here...let us know about it! Give us a review and we may feature your recipe in the next book.

CHAPTER 16:
BREAKFAST:

Tired of the same old morning meals??? Well jump out of bed and jump into this chapter that is full of protein and morning munchies! We will turn your head with some of these! If you're not a breakfast in the morning person...then this chapter is served any time of the day! So, ladies and gentlemen...Get Your Grub On! And "Top of the Morning", "Afternoon" and "Evening" to you, because, "Breakfast is Now Being Served!

BABY SPINACH AND GARLIC SCRAMBLED EGGS

This is an easy skillet dish for busy mornings. Here, you can combine baby spinach with your eggs for a healthy fast meal that will be a hit at the breakfast table.

Prep Time: 15 Minutes
Cook Time: 15 Minutes
Servings: 4

INGREDIENTS

12 oz. baby spinach leaves (package is fine as well)
½ cup chopped onion
1 clove of garlic (chopped)
4 tbsp. heavy cream

8 eggs, beaten
pinch of salt
pinch of pepper
½ tsp. dried thyme leaves
2 tbsp. grated parmesan cheese

DIRECTIONS

> Prepare: in a mixing bowl beat with eggs with cream, salt, pepper and thyme.
> Add the spinach, onion and garlic to a non-stick skillet and cook for 7 minutes.
> Put the egg mixture to the skillet and cook for 5 minutes toss the eggs till done.
> Garnish with cheese and serve.

NUTRITIONAL FACTS:

Serving Size 211 g, Amount Per Serving, Calories 233Calories from Fat 153, Total Fat 17.0g, Saturated Fat 7.7g, Trans Fat 0.0g, Cholesterol 355mg, Sodium 279mg, Potassium 636mg, Total Carbohydrates 6.0g, Dietary Fiber 2.3g, Sugars 1.7g, Protein 15.8g

Vitamin A 174%, Vitamin C 42%, Calcium 20%, Iron 23%, Nutrition Grade A, Based on a 2000 calorie diet

NUTRITIONAL ANALYSIS / GOOD POINTS

Low in sugar, High in manganese, High in phosphorus, High in riboflavin, Very high in selenium, Very high in vitamin A, High in vitamin C

A PLAY ON QUICHE

This egg dish is one of my favorites. My mother used to bake many different types of quiches growing up. This is a fast and easy way to keep that traditional alive for my family.

Prep Time: 10 Minutes
Cook Time: 10 Minutes
Servings: 4

INGREDIENTS

8 strips bacon (cut in half)
3/4 lb. asparagus (1 bunch)
Kosher salt
Freshly ground black pepper
6 eggs

1 cup heavy cream
2 tbsp. chopped chives
9 oz. frozen puff pastry (1 sheet,
thawed in refrigerator overnight)

DIRECTIONS

> Prepare eggs in a mixing bowl with cream, ½ tsp. black pepper and chives.
> Microwave bacon strips in for 3 minutes.
> In a non-stick skillet season asparagus with salt and pepper. Cook for 3 minutes, until soft.
> Roll out puff pastry on floured surface and cut into 4 equal squares.
> Place each cut out piece into the skillet.
> Place egg mixture, bacon and asparagus into the skillet.
> Bake at 350 degrees for 30 minutes.
> Serve.

NUTRITIONAL FACTS:

Serving Size 284 g, Amount Per Serving, Calories 772, Calories from Fat 522, Total Fat 58.0g, Saturated Fat 20.4g, Trans Fat 0.0g, Cholesterol 328mg, Sodium 1181mg, Potassium 541mg, Total Carbohydrates 34.0g, Dietary Fiber 2.8g, Sugars 2.6g, Protein 29.6g

Vitamin A 30%, Vitamin C 10%, Calcium 9%, Iron 29%, Nutrition Grade B-, Based on a 2000 calorie diet

NUTRITIONAL ANALYSIS / GOOD POINTS

Low in sugar, High in selenium

COUNTRY STYLE POTATO OMELET SKILLET

Peppers, onions and ham and potatoes all in one place. Forget about flipping the perfect omelet and let the oven do all the work for you.

Prep Time: 20 Minutes
Cook Time: 20 Minutes
Servings: 4

INGREDIENTS

8 large eggs
4 ounces diced deli ham
2 diced bell peppers
1 diced onion
1 tsp. kosher salt

1 tsp. freshly ground pepper
2 tbsp. unsalted butter
3 cups frozen shredded hash browns
4 ounces grated smoked gouda cheese
1/2 cup scallions (chopped)

DIRECTIONS

> To prepare the eggs, add them to large mixing bowl and whisk them until foamy.
> in a non-stick skillet add the ham, bell peppers, onions, salt and pepper and cook for 6 minutes.
> Add to the bowl with eggs.
> Add the hash browns to the skillet and cook for 5 minutes.
> Put the egg mixture over the hash browns and then add the skillet to the oven.
> Cook for 4 minutes.
> Add the cheese and scallions and cook for 2 more minutes.
> Garnish with scallions and serve.

NUTRITIONAL FACTS:

Serving Size 382 g, Amount Per Serving, Calories 686Calories from Fat 367, Total Fat 40.8g, Saturated Fat 14.8g, Cholesterol 436mg, Sodium 1770mg, Potassium 1132mg, Total Carbohydrates 51.0g, Dietary Fiber 6.4g, Sugars 7.1g, Protein 29.1g

Vitamin A 56%, Vitamin C 161%, Calcium 30%, Iron 19%, Nutrition Grade B, Based on a 2000 calorie diet

NUTRITIONAL ANALYSIS / GOOD POINTS

High in selenium, Very high in vitamin C

ITALIAN STYLE EGGS AND ELECTRIC SKILLETCETTA

Making eggs into comfort food? Adding electric pancetta, basil and sauce to these eggs will remind you of Mom's cooking minus the meatballs.

Prep Time: 35 Minutes
Cook Time: 35 Minutes
Servings: 4

INGREDIENTS

1 diced medium onion
2 chopped cloves of garlic
1 oz. chopped electric pancetta
2 cups prepared marinara sauce
4 large eggs

6 large fresh basil leaves, torn into small pieces
1 tbsp. grated parmesan cheese
¼ tsp. freshly ground pepper
4 toasted slices whole-wheat country bread

DIRECTIONS

> In a non-stick skillet combine onion, garlic and electric pancetta. Cook for 5 minutes.
> Add marinara sauce and bring down to a simmer
> Crack an egg and gently add it to the skillet.
> Season with basil, cover and cook for 8 minutes.
> Garnish with cheese and pepper and serve with bread.

NUTRITIONAL FACTS:

Amount Per Serving, Calories 314, Calories from Fat 117, Total Fat 13.0g, Saturated Fat 4.1g, Trans Fat 0.2g, Cholesterol 199mg, Sodium 914mg, Potassium 622mg, Total Carbohydrates 32.7g, Dietary Fiber 5.8g, Sugars 14.2g, Protein 16.4g

Vitamin A 18%, Vitamin C 8%, Calcium 13%, Iron 15%, Nutrition Grade B+, Based on a 2000 calorie diet

NUTRITIONAL ANALYSIS / GOOD POINTS

High in niacin, High in selenium

HOMESTYLE BACON PEPPER POTATO BREAKFAST FILLER

When you can't choose between sausage or bacon, toast or muffins. This breakfast skillet has it all.

Prep Time: 45 Minutes
Cook Time: 45 Minutes
Servings: 4

INGREDIENTS

2 lbs. potatoes (cubed)
½ lb. bacon

1 bell pepper (diced green)
1 teaspoon crushed red peppers

DIRECTIONS -

> -In a pot bring potatoes to boil; cooking for 12 minutes.
> - In a non-stick skillet cook the bacon for 5 minutes. Set aside when finished.
> Add potatoes to the electric skillet and stir in peppers, onion, crushed red peppers and mushrooms. Cook for 5 minutes. (Making sure they start to turn a little brown)
> Stir in bacon, cover with cheese and cook eggs together until eggs are done cooking and set.
> Garnish and serve.
> Cook eggs to your preferred style. Place potatoes in a large serving dish, and top with eggs.
> Serve

NUTRITIONAL FACTS:

Amount Per Serving, Calories 474, Calories from Fat 217, Total Fat 24.1g37%, Saturated Fat 7.9g, Trans Fat 0.0g, Cholesterol 62mg, Sodium 1325mg, Potassium 1315mg, Total Carbohydrates 38.5g, Dietary Fiber 6.2g, Sugars 3.9g, Protein 25.1g

Vitamin A 23%, Vitamin C 138%, Calcium 3%, Iron 12%, Nutrition Grade B, Based on a 2000 calorie diet

NUTRITIONAL ANALYSIS / GOOD POINTS

Low in sugar, High in selenium, Very high in vitamin C

SPICY BACON AND HASH BROWN POTATOES SKILLET

This skillet adds a little heat to your palate. By combining chilies in the dish, you have decided to kick it up a notch, especially in the flavor scale.

Prep Time: 30 Minutes
Cook Time: 30 Minutes
Servings: 4

INGREDIENTS

¾ lb. chopped bacon
3 cups hash brown potatoes
(refrigerated cooked shredded)
3 Large eggs

4oz green chilies (1 can)
¾ cup shredded cheddar cheese
1 chopped medium tomato

DIRECTIONS

> Prepare eggs in a mixing bowl with chilies.
> In a non-stick skillet cook bacon for 7 minutes.
> Add potatoes and cook for 10 more minutes.
> Put eggs over potatoes and cook for 10 minutes.
> Add cheese and tomato, cover and cook for 2 more minutes. When cheese is melted...it's done!
> Garnish and serve.

NUTRITIONAL FACTS:

Amount Per Serving, Calories 924, Calories from Fat 549, Total Fat 61.0g, Saturated Fat 19.5g, Trans Fat 0.0g, Cholesterol 255mg, Sodium 2664mg, Potassium 1298mg. Total Carbohydrates 46.0g, Dietary Fiber 4.1g. Sugars 3.9g, Protein 45.3g

Vitamin A 16%, Vitamin C 47%, Calcium 20%, Iron 15%, Nutrition Grade C, Based on a 2000 calorie diet

NUTRITIONAL ANALYSIS / GOOD POINTS

Low in sugar, High in selenium

FOR THE LOVE OF SEASONED BREAKFAST POTATOES SKILLET

If you love potatoes, especially for breakfast, then this is the recipe for you. This recipe was created for the spud lover and wanted to bring it to the main stage.

Prep Time: 40 Minutes
Cook Time: 40 Minutes
Servings: 6

INGREDIENTS

5 russet potatoes (peeled)
1 ½ tsp. kosher salt
¼ tbs. freshly ground black pepper

1 cup scallions (2 bunches diced)
1 tsp. sea salt (coarse)

DIRECTIONS

> Season potatoes with salt and pepper.
> Place half of the potatoes in a non-stick skillet, add scallions and top with more potatoes.
> Cook for 12 minutes.
> Flip over and cook for 12 more minutes.
> Garnish with sea salt and scallions and serve.

NUTRITIONAL FACTS:

Amount Per Serving, Calories 129, Calories from Fat 2, Total Fat 0.2g, Cholesterol 0mg, Sodium 907mg, Potassium 772mg, Total Carbohydrates 29.3g, Dietary Fiber 4.8g, Sugars 2.4g, Protein 3.3g

Vitamin A 4%, Vitamin C 64%, Calcium 3%, Iron 7%, Nutrition Grade A, Based on a 2000 calorie diet

NUTRITIONAL ANALYSIS / GOOD POINTS

Very low in saturated fat, No cholesterol, High in dietary fiber, High in potassium, High in vitamin B6, Very high in vitamin C

BLISSFUL B.L.T. BISCUITS

The famous B.L.T. is no longer just dedicated to lunch. Bacon is already used in breakfast, can be in every other meal truthfully, and tomatoes and kale (the lettuce substitute) are just as adaptable. Add an egg and stick in between a sliced biscuit and you have a great start to your day!

Prep Time: 10 Minutes
Cook Time: 30 Minutes
Servings: 8

INGREDIENTS

1 can (16.3 oz.) Pillsbury™ Grands!™ Homestyle refrigerated buttermilk biscuits
8 slices thick-cut maple bacon
1/4 cup packed brown sugar

8 pasteurized eggs*
1 handful fresh kale leaves
1 large avocado, pitted, peeled and sliced
1 large tomato, cut into 8 slices

DIRECTIONS

› Place a can of refrigerated buttermilk biscuits on the skillet, the sides can touch so don't worry about them touching. Bake at 325 degrees until biscuits start to turn golden brown, which can range anywhere from 22-24 minutes.
› Raise the temperature to 400°F and place the bacon strips on foil atop the skillet. In a separate mixing container, mix together the brown sugar with a tablespoon of water and then coat each slice of bacon. Bake until crisp, about 20 minutes, then use paper towels or something to sop up or drain the bacon.
› Next, it's time to bring the sandwiches together. Slice open each biscuit, splitting evenly across the middle.
› You may cook the eggs to your liking.
› Work in layers from the bottom biscuit up: kale leaves, avocado, tomato, egg, then bacon. Put the top biscuit on and your sandwich is ready.
› This is what you call "breakfast, lunch or dinner!" Yummm… ;)

NUTRITIONAL FACTS:

Serving Size 113 g, Amount Per Serving, Calories 246, Calories from Fat 86, Total Fat 9.6g, Saturated Fat 1.4g, Trans Fat 0.0g, Cholesterol 1mg, Sodium 622mg, Potassium 329mg, Total Carbohydrates 36.3g, Dietary Fiber 1.4g, Sugars 7.0g, Protein 4.6g

Vitamin A 91%, Vitamin C 62%, Calcium 7%, Iron 14%, Nutrition Grade B+, Based on a 2000 calorie diet

NUTRITIONAL ANALYSIS / GOOD POINTS
Very low in cholesterol, High in phosphorus, Very high in vitamin A, Very high in vitamin C

A BUNNY'S FLUFFY BREAKFAST DELIGHT

The old cliché is that rabbits enjoy carrots, but they aren't the only ones, especially when offered in cake form. These cookie bars are hearty and full of great ingredients to balance out the "cake" or "cookie" label: apples, raisins, and oats! The Doc would approve.

Prep Time: 20 Minutes
Cook Time: 40 Minutes
Servings: 14

INGREDIENTS

1 package refrigerated sugar cookies
1 3/4 cups quick-cooking oats
1/2 cup cranberry raisins.
1 teaspoon ground cinnamon

3/4 cup chopped carrots (1 medium)
2 cups chopped Honey Crisp apples
2 eggs

DIRECTIONS

⟩ Bring refrigerated sugar cookies to room temperature.
⟩ After breaking up the cookie dough, mix in oats, cranberry raisins, and ground cinnamon until blended in a mixing container.
⟩ Using the pulse option on a food processor, beat the chopped carrots for 15-20 seconds then add the apples and beat for another 10-15 seconds.
⟩ Break the eggs into the cookie dough mixture then add the carrots and apples. Mix very well before placing all the batter into electric skillet.
⟩ Bake at 375 degrees for 30 minutes. Afterwards, let stand for 10 minutes to cool.

NUTRITIONAL FACTS:

Serving Size 79 g, Amount Per Serving, Calories 166, Calories from Fat 24, Total Fat 2.7g, Saturated Fat 0.6g, Trans Fat 0.0g, Cholesterol 23mg, Sodium 289mg, Potassium 122mg, Total Carbohydrates 30.3g, Dietary Fiber 2.6g, Sugars 3.8g, Protein 5.3g

Vitamin A 20%, Vitamin C 3%, Calcium 7%, Iron 12%, Nutrition Grade A-, Based on a 2000 calorie diet

NUTRITIONAL ANALYSIS / GOOD POINTS

Low in saturated fat, High in manganese, High in selenium, High in vitamin A, High in vitamin B6

SWEET AND SOFT FRENCH TOAST FINGERS

Cinnamon, vanilla, maple syrup, and yogurt; there's not much else to say except for the fact that these French toast sticks will be a hit with the entire family. There is a double dose of ingredients with the toast and the sauce so there will be plenty of flavor to go around!

Prep Time: 5 Minutes
Cook Time: 4 Minutes
Servings: 2

INGREDIENTS

4 Eggs
½ Cup Vanilla Nonfat Greek yogurt
1/4 tsp. powdered sugar
¼ tsp. Ground Cinnamon
4 slices wide-loaf day-old bread

SAUCE

¾ Cup Vanilla Nonfat Greek yogurt
¼ Cup electric pancake syrup
1/8 tsp. Ground cinnamon

DIRECTIONS

> Create sauce by combining Greek yogurt, electric pancake syrup, and cinnamon.
> Using a separate dish, beat eggs and blend in yogurt, powdered sugar, and cinnamon.
> Slice each piece of bread into 4 sticks. Immerse each side of each stick in the egg mixture.
> Heat nonstick skillet over medium heat. Cook each bread stick, in batches if necessary, for 1-2 minutes on each side, reducing the heat slightly if needed. There should be no liquid remains visible. If needed, clean the skillet between batches.

NUTRITIONAL FACTS:

Serving Size 299 g, Amount Per Serving, Calories 377, Calories from Fat 101, Total Fat 11.2g, Saturated Fat 4.4g, Trans Fat 0.0g, Cholesterol 337mg, Sodium 385mg, Potassium 502mg, Total Carbohydrates 45.3g, Dietary Fiber 0.6g, Sugars 21.0g, Protein 21.2g

Vitamin A 10%, Vitamin C 2%, Calcium 36%, Iron 14%, Nutrition Grade B, Based on a 2000 calorie diet

NUTRITIONAL ANALYSIS / GOOD POINTS

High in phosphorus, High in riboflavin, High in selenium

PEPPERY MINCED GARLIC HOME FRIES ON THE STOVE

Nothing beats a hearty home-cooked meal, and considering breakfast is the most important meal of the day and usually consumed at home, there is good reason to begin your day with energy from classic home fries. Potatoes, onions, and spices will get you going in no time!

Prep Time: 20 Minutes
Cook Time: 20 Minutes
Servings: 4

INGREDIENTS

*1 1/2 pounds Russet potatoes (about
3 medium or 2 large potatoes)
2 tablespoons olive oil, divided
1 tablespoon unsalted butter
1 medium onion, diced*

*2 cloves minced garlic
1 teaspoon smoked paprika
1 teaspoon parsley
Pinch of Salt
Pinch of Pepper*

DIRECTIONS

> Cut the washed potatoes into half-inch squares. Cover with cold water in an electric skillet and season with a pinch of salt. After the water boils, cook for 1-2 minutes or until soft.

> Add 1 tablespoon of olive oil in a skillet over medium heat and cook the onions and garlic for 5 minutes, occasionally stirring, using season salt and pepper to season.

> After draining the potatoes, let stand for 5 minutes to cool.

> Add the remaining olive oil and butter in another skillet over medium heat. Season the potatoes with salt and pepper and toss them around in the oil, then cook them for 8-10 minutes, spreading them out in the electric skillet. Batches are suggested depending on the size of the skillet or size of the cubes.

> Mix in the cooked onions and garlic, parsley, and paprika to the skillet and continue mixing the potatoes.

> Serve immediately after turning off the heat and removing the electric skillet.

Note: to make this a special treat...sprinkle a little cheese over top of potatoes and let stand 5 min till cheese melts. Mmmmmmm ;)

NUTRITIONAL FACTS:

Serving Size 213 g, Amount Per Serving, Calories 219, Calories from Fat 92, Total Fat 10.2g, Saturated Fat 2.9g, Cholesterol 8mg, Sodium 614mg, Potassium 760mg, Total Carbohydrates 30.4g, Dietary Fiber 5.0g, Sugars 3.2g, Protein 3.4g

Vitamin A 8%, Vitamin C 61%, Calcium 3%, Iron 7%, Nutrition Grade B, Based on a 2000 calorie diet

NUTRITIONAL ANALYSIS / GOOD POINTS

Good points, Low in cholesterol, Very high in vitamin C

MOIST & HEARTY OATMEAL BLUEBERRY MUFFINS

Blueberry muffins are very recognizable in the breakfast world, very simple, and very popular despite their humbleness. They never were missing anything, but to add a little more substance, oats provide an extra kick to this already appealing course!

Prep Time: 20 Minutes
Cook Time: 1 Hour & 45 Minutes
Servings: 12

INGREDIENTS

1 1/2 cups all-purpose flour
1 cup quick-cooking oats
2 1/4 teaspoons baking powder
1 teaspoon coarse salt
1/2 teaspoon ground cinnamon
3/4 cup sugar
2 large eggs

1 stick unsalted butter, melted and cooled
1/2 cup whole milk

1 cups blueberries
1/4 cup cranberries

DIRECTIONS

> Preheat electric skillet at 350 degrees. Place baking cups into the skillet.
> Mix together flour, oats, baking powder, salt, and cinnamon in a mixing container.
> Using a different mixing container, mix together sugar, eggs, butter, and milk.
> Combine both mixtures, then add blueberries and cranberries to the blend.
> Fill each cup a quarter of the way up, and keep even if there is extra batter. Bake for 20 minutes. Let the muffins sit in the electric skillet for 5 minutes before removing.
> Note: Sprinkle a few pinches of brown sugar and a drop of vanilla on top of each muffin before putting them in the oven! "A sure way to make you smile!" ;)

FRESH OMELETTES, OH MY!

Omelets are a breakfast and brunch basic, and they are incredibly easy to make! Besides being simple and classic, the breakfast dish is also very versatile and a variety of ingredients can be used to cook up what you crave the most. Onions, peppers, mushrooms, cheese, scallions, pepperoni, whatever you want, you can't go wrong.

Prep Time: 15 Minutes
Cook Time: 15 Minutes
Servings: 1

INGREDIENTS

2-3 eggs
Salt and pepper, to taste
2 cloves minced garlic

1/4 cup chopped onion
2-3 tsp. butter (can use less with nonstick electric skillet)

DIRECTIONS

> Beat the 2-3 eggs and season as desired.
> Add butter to a fry electric skillet over medium to medium-high heat. Make sure the bottom and sides are coated as it melts.
> Add the egg mixture and allow the eggs to set up for 30 seconds; sliding the electric skillet back and forth very gently before let it set for just another minute.
> Lift the edge of the egg mixture carefully with spatula and slant the electric skillet, allowing the liquid on top to touch the surface of the electric skillet. (You can also use a fork or something flat to achieve this result) Repeat this step around the entire omelet making sure the eggs are set up evenly around the omelet. If the omelet is moving around easily, but staying together, it's ready.
> With this electric skillet, it should be very easy to slide right out of the electric skillet! ;)

NUTRITIONAL FACTS:

Serving Size 132 g, Amount Per Serving, Calories 214, Calories from Fat 148, Total Fat 16.4g, Saturated Fat 7.6g, Cholesterol 348mg, Sodium 180mg, Potassium 187mg, Total Carbohydrates 5.4g, Dietary Fiber 0.8g, Sugars 2.0g, Protein 11.9g, Vitamin A 13%, Vitamin C 7%, Calcium 7%, Iron 10%, Nutrition Grade B-, Based on a 2000 calorie diet

NUTRITIONAL ANALYSIS / GOOD POINTS

High in riboflavin, Very high in selenium

SAVORY SUPERFOOD FRITTATA

This is primarily a breakfast dish, but is easy enough to make for lunch or dinner, however, let's get the day started off right. Another Superfood emerges in kale, and though sweet potato may seem like an odd addition to breakfast, it blends perfectly with this tasty dish!

Prep Time: 20 Minutes
Cook Time: 10 Minutes
Servings: 4

INGREDIENTS

6 large eggs
1 c. half-and-half
1 tsp. Kosher salt
½ tsp. Freshly ground pepper
1/4 tsp. cinnamon
2 c. sweet potatoes
2 tbsp. olive oil

1 c. spinach (firmly packed chopped)
1 c. kale (firmly packed chopped)
½ small red onion
2 clove garlic
3 oz. goat cheese

DIRECTIONS

⟩ Combine the eggs, half-and-half, salt, pepper, and cinnamon after you preheat the skillet to 350 degrees F.

⟩ Add 1 tablespoon oil to a nonstick skillet over medium and sauté potatoes for 8-10 minutes. After removal, cover them with foil to keep warm. Using the same skillet, cook spinach, onion, and garlic in another tablespoon of oil for 3-4 minutes; add the potatoes back in and put the egg mixture over everything. Cook for 3 minutes then dust the top with goat cheese.

⟩ Bake 10-14 minutes and you're all ready to go.

⟩ Quick, tasty and fun for everyone! ;)

NUTRITIONAL FACTS:

Serving Size 276 g, Amount Per Serving, Calories 447Calories from Fat 263, Total Fat 29.2g, Saturated Fat 12.9g, Trans Fat 0.0g, Cholesterol 324mg, Sodium 805mg, Potassium 948mg, Total Carbohydrates 28.2g, Dietary Fiber 3.9g, Sugars 1.9g, Protein 19.8g, Vitamin A 87%, Vitamin C 61%, Calcium 34%, Iron 16%, Nutrition Grade B, Based on a 2000 calorie diet

NUTRITIONAL ANALYSIS / GOOD POINTS

Low in sugar, High in vitamin A, High in vitamin C

THE ESSENTIAL TOASTED BREAKFAST SANDWICH

Simple is probably the most underrated characteristic in recipes. Sometimes we just need to get back to basics because the best lies within. Bacon, eggs, cheese, and toast all in one! Fruit makes the perfect garnish, and everything you need is right in front of you (coffee optional, if needed).

Prep Time: 4 Minutes
Cook Time: 6 Minutes
Servings: 2

INGREDIENTS

2 Eggs
2 tbsp. milk or water
3 tsp. butter, room temperature, divided

4 slices bread of choice
2 slices cheese of choice
4 slices fully-cooked bacon
1/4 tsp. basil

DIRECTIONS

> Whisk together eggs, milk, salt and pepper.
> Melt 1 teaspoon butter in a large nonstick skillet over medium heat. Add the egg mixture, and carefully mix back and forth with a spatula just for a minute, just until they start to set up. Cook until thick and there is no visible liquid to the eggs & there is no stirring necessary. Clean the skillet before the next step.
> Butter one side of each slice of bread. Grill the bread, buttered side against the surface of the skillet, top each with scrambled eggs, cheese and bacon. Put the other slices of on top of the ingredients, with the buttered side up this time.
> Cook 2-4 minutes, flipping the sandwich halfway through.
> Makes a yummy treat for breakfast, lunch or dinner... ;)

NUTRITIONAL FACTS:

Serving Size 225 g, Amount Per Serving, Calories 737, Calories from Fat 412, Total Fat 45.8g, Saturated Fat 19.4g, Trans Fat 0.0g, Cholesterol 272mg, Sodium 2095mg, Potassium 491mg, Total Carbohydrates 39.6g, Dietary Fiber 1.8g, Sugars 4.4g, Protein 39.7g

Vitamin A 14%, Vitamin C 0%, Calcium 36%, Iron 25%, Nutrition Grade C-, Based on a 2000 calorie diet

NUTRITIONAL ANALYSIS / GOOD POINTS

Low in sugar, High in selenium, Total Fat: 23 g, Saturated fat: 11 g, Polyunsaturated fat: 2 g, Monounsaturated fat: 6 g, Cholesterol: 239 mg, Sodium: 698 mg, Carbohydrates: 24 g, Dietary Fiber: 4 g, Protein: 23 g

Vitamin A: 777.6 IU, Vitamin D: 52.7 IU, Folate: 52.7 mcg, Calcium: 256.9 mg, Iron: 2.4 mg, Choline: 156.7 mg

"Bonus Chapter 17:"
MOUTH WATERING MARINADES!

10 HAND SELECTED MOUTHWATERING
MARINADES FOR MEATS:

If you want your meat to be an amazingly "High Flavored, Smack in the Mouth" taste that you've never experienced before...then we have "**this bonus section**" for you! These are the 10 favorite marinades that we pulled out of "The Play Book" just for you! Every pulsating taste of bliss that you'll ever want on your meat is right here at your fingertips!

Someone once asked me if I marinade my meats! My response was..." ABSOLUTELY!" This is a regular practice for me and I take pride in this process. My theory on this one is..." If you have a piece of meat, then it better be soaking in some delicious juices that will have you begging for more. Now...take your meal and "Dive in Head First" to these delicious meat soaking juices! ;)

APPLE CIDER HOT MUSTARD GARLIC MARINADE:

INGREDIENTS:

1/2 cup apple cider vinegar
1/2 cup dry mustard
4 tbsp. of garlic juice

1/3 cup sugar
1 egg
1 cup mayonnaise

DIRECTIONS:

> Combine these ingredients, except the garlic and mayonnaise, in a blender for best results!
> Prepare and warm up these ingredients in an electric skillet on medium heat.
> You will start to see the sauce get thicker.
> After it thickens from the heat mix in 4 tbsp. of garlic juice 1 cup mayonnaise and stir the mixture!

CINNAMON BASIL HONEY MARINADE W/ GARLIC

INGREDIENTS:

1/2 cup onion (minced)
1/4 cup fresh lemon juice
1/4 cup avocado oil
2 tbsp. low sodium soy sauce
2 cloves garlic (crushed or minced)

1 tbsp. ginger (grated fresh)
2 tbsp. honey
1/2 tsp. cinnamon
1 tsp. basil
2 tsp. chopped fresh parsley

DIRECTIONS:

> Combine all of these ingredients together in a blender for best results!

WHITE WINE JALAPEÑO/CAYENNE MARINADE

INSTRUCTIONS:

2 1/2 cups white wine (dry)
1/2 teaspoon cayenne pepper
1 jalapeno pepper (minced)
1 teaspoon onion powder

1/2 cup soy sauce
1/2 teaspoon garlic powder
1/2 tsp. parsley
1/2 tsp. fresh ground pepper

DIRECTIONS:

> Combine all of these ingredients together in a blender for best results!

RED WINE SWEET CAJUN MARINADE

INSTRUCTIONS:

1/3 cup soy sauce & 1/2 cup red wine
2 tablespoons Cajun seasoning
2 tablespoons minced garlic
2 tablespoons brown sugar
1/2 teaspoon cinnamon

1 tablespoon tomato paste
1 teaspoon freshly ground black pepper
1 splash of lemon juice

DIRECTIONS:

> Combine all of these ingredients together in a blender for best results!

LEMON PEPPER BASIL MARINADE

INGREDIENTS:

2/3 cup lemon juice
3 oz. water
2 teaspoons chicken bouillon (granules)

2 cloves garlic (minced)
1 teaspoon pepper (fresh ground)
1/2 teaspoon basil

DIRECTIONS:

> Combine all of these ingredients together in a blender for best results!

MOUTH WATERING MEXICAN STYLE MARINADE

INGREDIENTS:

1/4 cup lime juice
1/4 cup avocado oil
1/3 cup water
1 tablespoon vinegar
2 teaspoons soy sauce (low sodium)

2 teaspoons Worcestershire sauce
1 clove garlic, minced
1/2 teaspoon chili powder
1/2 teaspoon beef bouillon paste
1/2 teaspoon ground cumin

1/2 teaspoon cilantro
1/2 teaspoon dried oregano

1/4 teaspoon ground black pepper

DIRECTIONS:

> Combine all of these ingredients together in a blender for best results!

PINEAPPLE RASPBERRY MEAT TWISTER MARINADE

INGREDIENTS:

1/2 cup raspberry preserves
1/2 teaspoon lemon juice
1/2 cup pineapple juice
1/2 cup soy sauce

2 tablespoons rice vinegar
1/2 teaspoon minced garlic
1/2 teaspoon dried basil

DIRECTIONS:

> Combine all of these ingredients together in a blender for best results!

ITALIAN MEAT MARINATING MAGNIFIER

INGREDIENTS:

1/2 cup Italian dressing
1/2 teaspoon lemon juice
1/2 teaspoon minced garlic

1/2 teaspoon dried basil
1/2 teaspoon Tabasco sauce

DIRECTIONS:

> Combine all of these ingredients together in a blender for best results!

MILD MARINADE SEAFOOD SOAKER

INSTRUCTIONS:

1/2 cup onion (minced)
1/4 cup fresh lemon juice
1/8 cup avocado oil

1/8 cup butter (almond butter best)
2 tsp. chopped fresh parsley

DIRECTIONS:

> Combine all of these ingredients together in a blender for best results!

WHITE WINE SEAFOOD GARLIC MARINADE

INSTRUCTIONS:

2 1/2 cups white wine (dry)
1/8 cup avocado oil
1 tbsp. Old Bay Seasoning

1/4 cup fresh lemon juice
2 tsp. chopped parsley (fresh)
2 tsp. paprika

DIRECTIONS:

> Combine all of these ingredients together in a blender for best results!

DID YOU ENJOY THIS PUBLICATION? HERE'S WHAT YOU DO NOW...

If you were pleased with our book then please leave us a review on Amazon! In the world of an author who writes books independently, your reviews are not only touching but important so that we know you like the material we have prepared for "YOU" our audience! So, leave us a review...we would love to see that you enjoyed our book!

If for any reason that you were less than happy with your experience then send me an email at feedback@HealthyLifestyleRecipes.org and let me know how we can better your experience. We always come out with a few volumes of our books and will possibly be able to address some of your concerns. Do keep in mind that we strive to do our best to give you the highest quality of what "we the independent authors" pour our heart and tears into.

Again...I really appreciate your purchase and thank you for your many great reviews and comments! With a warm heart!
~Shannon McMillian...xoxo :)

A LITTLE ABOUT THE AUTHOR
OF THIS BOOK

Shannon McMillian is a highly trained, self-taught, private gourmet chef that has enjoyed her craft in the kitchens of many celebrities and exclusive events of Southern California. She enjoys creating new recipes for an array of categories and writes recipes and books from her heart and soul to share with you!

FREE BOOKS!!!

New Books, Pro Cooking Tips, & Recipes
Sent to Your Email

For our current readers...if you like receiving free books, pro cooking tips & recipes to add to your collection, then this is for you! This is for promoting our material to our current members so you can review our new books and give us feed back when we launch new books we are publishing! This helps us determine how we can make our books better for you, our audience! Just go to the url below and leave your name and email. We will send you a complimentary book about once a month.

Get My Free Book

www.HealthyLifestyleRecipes.org/FreeBook2Review

OTHER BOOKS WE HIGHLY RECOMMEND!

>> C lick the links below to Taste the Deliciousness! Enjoy! ☺ <<

Crisper Basket Recipe Cookbook is one of our favorite stories yet! You will love and enjoy all of these mouthwatering ways to crisp up that food without using grease or oils because you make meals in your very own oven. Air Fryer style cooking recipes right in the comfort of your own home! Great gift for anyone to enjoy!
https://www.amazon.com/Crisper-Basket-Recipe-Cookbook-Multi-Purpose/dp/1974510565

If you are looking for amazing foods that go great for any occasion then you should check out **"Ceramic Titanium Cookbook"** by Sasha Hassler & Allison August! There are many delicious foods and desserts that can be made in this non-stick ceramic titanium fry pan. With over 99 different recipes you will become a large fan of this great Amazon selling cookbook! Click the link below to get yours!
http://www.amazon.com/Ceramic-Titanium-Cookbook-Delicious-Nutritious/dp/1545047995

Crisper Tray Recipe Cookbook is the best way to keep that food crispy! This Air Fryer Style food tray will fit right in your very own oven and give you the crisp you've always been looking for. The clean and healthy way to cook this year! We've got you covered with all of the crispy foods you can air fry in the convenience of your own home! Enjoy!
https://www.amazon.com/Crisper-Tray-Recipe-Cookbook-Revolutionary/dp/1976321212

Electric Skillet Cookbook Complete Recipe Notes:

Electric Skillet Cookbook Complete Recipe Notes: